Read what these company presidents have to say about Leading Under Pressure...

Brian Dyson—Former president and CEO of Coca-Cola Enterprises

"I believe feeling pressure is far more pervasive than we realize. You may be in charge of a major public company and be subjected to the pressure of 'enhancing shareholder value,' but your spouse may feel similar pressure to prepare your children for life. So we all need to understand this reality."

"While being the head of a large international corporation is a visible example of leading under pressure, the same nerve-wracking feeling will be visited on an entrepreneur struggling to make payroll."

"I was always able to multi-task, to juggle more balls than normal; but I also grew my ability to do this. The danger is to become overloaded—to be beaten down by the pressure of too much on your plate."

Donna Shalala—President of University of Miami and former Secretary of Health and Human Services under President Clinton

"I once told my staff that the president of the United States hired us for our judgment and not for our stamina."

"I think that if you have high-pressure and high-profile jobs, people forget that working night and day doesn't mean you are going to make decisions better or quicker. Sometimes it's important to go home and sleep on it. You have to learn how to sleep on things and not let things keep you awake."

Gary Hoover—Entrepreneur; creator of Hoover's, Inc.; BOOKSTOP; and more

"There's no question that an awful lot of successful businesses and even successful artists come from constraints like past failures: the fact that you have limited resources, or the fact that you didn't make that big sale, or the fact that the venture capitalists wouldn't bank you."

"In a recent article I did in which I spoke about failure, the really important thing is that it's natural to go home and mope. But the real question is: do you mope for 30 minutes or 30 days...or 30 years!"

"The one thing that I like about entrepreneurship, one thing I love about retailing, is I can look in the mirror and say, 'Hey, if you succeed, it's you; if you fail, it's you.'"

Janet Vergis—Former president of Janssen, McNeil Pediatrics, and Ortho-McNeil Neurologics (CNS businesses for Johnson & Johnson)

"When you get into a leadership position, I don't think there is a day that you don't feel pressure—a big part of that is the need to make tough decisions. If I think about the really tough decisions I've had to make, they usually fall into one of two categories: decisions where not all the information is available or clear and there doesn't seem to be an obvious right or wrong; and decisions where the answer is apparent, but the *implementation* is difficult. It takes courage to make both types of decisions."

"There was the obvious pressure of needing to make our business goals despite the fact that we would have less people and resources, but the bigger difficulty for me was the human toll. A downsizing impacts not only the people we have to let go, but also the people who are left as 'survivors.'"

"Sure you can sleep on it—or perhaps better characterized in my case, stay awake because of it, but for big decisions I always try to bring in the expertise of others. Good decisions can't be made in a vacuum."

Gerry Czarnecki—President of O2 Media and former senior executive at IBM and Bank of America

"So much of what I've done is going into something that's broken and fixing it. First, going into a troubled situation where there is a great deal of stress, where things are broken, where I mean literally that things are not working right—where either the company is working its way to bankruptcy or if someone is in an operational nightmare that nobody thought they could get out of. The first thing that happens to the person when they take on that assignment, I don't care *what* they tell you, the first thing that happens is you get scared."

"Every single time that I went into a new job after that, where there was this firefight that I had to go face, the big first step was to step back and away from everything that was there and really drill down on two things."

Marsha Firestone—President of Women Presidents' Organization

"The lesson I learned is I didn't get what I thought I wanted. And so, I went out and did it myself...."

"The main lesson—pick yourself up, dust yourself off, and move ahead. Don't dwell on the devastation—keep going."

Leylani Cardoso—President of Bolzano Handbags

"Seven years ago, when my daughter had just been born and we found out she had special needs. All the while, my company lost two major contracts simultaneously. I think back and to this day, I say 'Wow, those were really tough times.'"

Fernando Parrado—Survivor and mastermind of a rescue after 72 days in Los Andes mountains

"I can tell you that I had all the pressure I could sustain in my life in my early years. Everything in the last 37 years has been a joy compared with what I went through, so any pressure in business is just issues, just simple things. The highest, most profound pressure I've ever felt is when you fight for your life and you know you're going to die."

"Everything I have faced afterwards, people say, 'How can you do so many things?' Because they are so easy compared to what I have done."

ExecutiveHealth.com's

LEADING
UNDER
PRESSURE

STRATEGIES TO AVOID BURNOUT, INCREASE ENERGY, AND IMPROVE YOUR WELL-BEING

Gabriela Cora, MD, MBA

Foreword by
William Yang, MD, MPH

CAREER
PRESS

Pompton Plains, N.J.

EXECUTIVEHEALTH.COM'S LEADING UNDER PRESSURE
EDITED AND TYPESET BY KARA KUMPEL
COVER DESIGN BY ROB JOHNSON/TOPROTYPE
PRINTED IN THE U.S.A. BY COURIER

To order this title, please call toll-free 1-800-CAREER-1 (NJ and Can-ada: 201-848-0310) to order using VISA or MasterCard, or for further information on books from Career Press.

The Career Press, Inc.
220 West Parkway, Unit 12
Pompton Plains, NJ 07444
www.careerpress.com

Library of Congress Cataloging-in-Publication Data

Corá, Gabriela.

ExecutiveHealth.com's leading under pressure : build your wealth without compromising your health / by Gabriela Cora.

p. cm.

Includes index.

ISBN 978-1-60163-128-2 -- ISBN 978-1-60163-721-5 (ebook) 1. Job stress. 2. Stress management. 3. Executives--Health

and hygience. I. Title. II. Title: Leading under pressure.

HF5548.85.C67 2010

158.7'2--dc22

2010025466

This book is dedicated to everyone who wants to experience the power of well-being while leading under pressure.

ACKNOWLEDGMENTS

I would like to express my deepest gratitude to the many people with whom I have worked and learned from to produce the ideas, concepts, and strategies that are presented in this book.

Also to my family: my husband, Eduardo, and my kids, Natalia and Marcos. My thanks to my parents, Rosita and Ettore; to Ellen and my siblings, Vanesa, Pablo, and Vero.

My special thanks to Natalia, for your assistance in transcribing the interviews and editing this work.

My deepest gratitude to the leaders who generously contributed to make this work a powerful source of inspiration to others who strive to lead under pressure: Leylani Cardoso, Gerry Czarnecki, Brian Dyson, Marsha Firestone, Gary Hoover, Nando Parrado, Donna Shalala, and Janet Vergis. Thank you, Doctors Michael Miller, MD, and Bill Yang, MD, for your contributions.

My special thanks to Bill and Steve Harrison for giving me the opportunity to meet the right people at the right time. To John Willig, my agent, and to Career Press and Michael Pye—thank you for believing in and supporting this project.

To my clients and my patients, you have trusted me to assist you throughout the last 20 years. You have been my source of inspiration, as I have learned from you.

CONTENTS

FOREWORD
by William Yang, MD, MPH

Stress is not new, nor is stress always negative. Stress for some serves as a motivator; for others it can help in adapting to new or changing situations in our work or life. In fact, it can help us accomplish things we may not have believed we could do, such as accomplishing a large project on time or performing beyond our limits in competition.

Acute stress in small doses can be exhilarating and exhausting at the same time, as in the case of speaking to large groups. However, when we experience frequent episodes of stress or chronic stress it can affect our physical and emotional health, our interpersonal relationships, our workplace productivity, and our enjoyment of our nonworkplace environment. Stress can result in presenteeism, absenteeism, and disability. At its worst stress can result in "burnout"—the exhaustion of all physical, emotional, and cognitive strength. Besides impacting individuals, stress can have an adverse effect on the environment of an entire organization.

Surveys indicate that more individuals are experiencing stress than in the past. Although stress can come from many different causes we seem to ascribe more stress to our jobs and our workplace.

Some of the reasons for this perception include:

☑ **Increasing workloads and longer work hours.** We are asked to be more productive and to do more with less. Restructuring, outsourcing, and change within organizations has become more the norm than the uncommon event.

☑ **High expectations.** The self-imposed expectations we place on ourselves and the expectations our managers and our peers demand from us.

☑ **Technology**—the double-edged sword. It can increase our productivity, or the lack of it can increase work hours. It can be a rapid way to communicate or a dreaded source of 24/7 access to clients, employees, or bosses.

- ☑ **The blurring of the work/personal boundary.** Working at work with coworkers and working afterward at home surrounded with family.

- ☑ **The fear of losing your job.**

Nonwork causes of stress include the desire and need for individuals to have a personal life, which can include being a supportive spouse, parent, and now often a caregiver to one's elders.

So how do we deal with stress and burnout, or, better yet, how do we prevent it?

Dr. Cora, a physician, trained mediator, wellness coach, and corporate consultant with an MBA, first noticed the phenomenon of stress and burnout in high-achieving business executives while she was in private practice. She began to see high-achieving businesspeople losing interest in their careers and developing symptoms ranging from mood disorders and physical symptoms to full burnout. As a result Dr. Cora developed deep insights into the challenges, stress-related problems, and health issues that affect today's corporate professionals and their organizations.

Realizing that we cannot avoid or eliminate stress, Dr. Cora then came up with the concept of "leading under pressure."

Early in her career Dr. Cora recognized the importance of prevention and she has made prevention an important element of "leading under pressure." She began to focus on helping businesspeople manage their stress, on providing insight to them, and on helping individuals prevent burnout. Dr. Cora's approach utilizes her knowledge and experience as a physician and as a business consultant to help individuals manage their stress and to improve and maximize their health.

Dr. Cora has developed a comprehensive approach that can be applied by individuals as well as by corporations. It provides a personalized approach to high productivity, life-work balance, maximizing health, and burnout prevention.

Bill Yang, MD, MPH
occupational physician, The Coca-Cola Company
Atlanta, 2010

PREFACE

☑ About 40% of workers report their job is "very or extremely stressful."
National Institute for Occupational Safety and Health, 2004

☑ Workers who must take time off work because of stress, anxiety, or a related disorder will be off the job for about 20 days.
Bureau of Labor Statistics, 2004

☑ Healthcare expenditures are nearly 50% greater for workers who report high levels of stress.
Journal of Occupational and Environmental Medicine, 2004

These reports are as relevant today as they were in 2004: Senior corporate executives ranked second to firefighters in the 2010 Jobs Rated report of most stressful jobs with high time pressure and high competition. Senior executives are expected to excel in many different fields at once, facing daily challenges to make far-reaching decisions that can affect hundreds or thousands of employees—and their company's bottom line. Millions around the world have striven to maximize their productivity, efficiency, and profitability *before* the recession. The global economic situation has raised stress to unimaginable levels.

If you feel like the professional juggler, multitasking and wishing for three extra pairs of hands, a new brain, or a couple of clones of yourself, this book is meant for you. **Leading Under Pressure** summarizes the many challenges executives, professionals, and entrepreneurs face in the current fast-paced financial craze, in which exceptional expectations in productivity and performance are the norm, but there is little guidance in how to do it all, perfectly well, and at once. And, of course, you are expected to succeed at everything in each and every aspect of your life: leading your team to achieve the best, contending against competing

13

groups, and enhancing your family's well-being—again, perfectly well, and at once!

Millions around the world are thinking, planning, and scheming to turn a 24-hour day into an endlessly productive working day, a repeating loop of "useful" time. Millions were already stretched too thin *before* the global recession. The problem is that busy business owners and executives face the daily quandary of finding new ways to thrive in order to achieve higher goals with increased competition, progressively limited resources, and the same manpower. Busy executives now experience the need to work many more hours to maintain their lifestyles. As they move up or across the corporate ladder, they find escalating challenges to remain level-headed, even-tempered, and able to balance all their difficulties all at once. Corporate executives find themselves needing to do more with less.

Leading Under Pressure represents my many hours of work as a corporate consultant, clinical researcher, and medical doctor. It summarizes and translates hours of interaction with patients, clients, and senior executive teams: assessing the challenging situation, identifying the obstacles, finding the opportunities, and strategically creating the solutions that will lead them to succeed. I have cited the most current studies from the most reliable sources done to date. Some of the cited studies may be seemingly older, when, in fact, they are the most current and from the most reliable sources. In this era of digital technology, I added Web links to these sources for your continued updates.

Most chapters start with a short vignette describing a specific situation that most executives and organizations face on a daily basis. These vignettes don't single out any one case that I have encountered but represent many of the typical situations I assess and advise on regularly.

This edition of **Leading Under Pressure** integrates lessons learned as shared by company CEOs, including Brian Dyson, past president of Coca-Cola Enterprises; Donna Shalala, president of the University of Miami and past Secretary of the Department of Health and Human Services during president Clinton's administration; Gary

Hoover, entrepreneur and founder of the concept of bookstores as a mall; Marsha Firestone, president of the Women Presidents' Organization; Janet Vergis, past president of Janssen Pharmaceuticals; Gerald Czarnecki, president of O2 Media; Leylani Cardoso, president of Bolzano Handbags; and the inspirational story of Fernando Parrado, mastermind of a survival expedition after his plane, carrying his family and rugby team, crashed in Los Andes mountains almost 40 years ago.

When reading **Leading Under Pressure**, you will benefit the most by taking time to better understand concepts regarding how stress impacts on your well-being, the multidimensional aspects of individual and organizational health, and the practical strategies to implement in your daily life. Pick one concept or strategy at a time as you focus on your path to continue to improve your performance and productivity while being healthy and well. The interviews in this edition serve to inspire you along your way of integrating work in life in full force and yet being well and experiencing joy at the core.

As a consultant, entrepreneur, wellness doctor and coach, researcher, author, speaker, spouse, and mother of two young adults, I can appreciate the incredible challenges and feats that you face in your daily responsibilities, as I continue to face and master these challenges myself. **Leading under Pressure** is a humble attempt to share the lessons learned, to provide for processed information applied in a rational and practical way, and to proactively design a solid foundation that will last a lifetime. **Leading Under Pressure** is intended to assist leading executives, busy professionals, and successful entrepreneurs as they continue to advance in their businesses and careers effectively and steadily. My purpose is to share as many tools with you as possible so that you can become your own guide, able to maximize your productivity and performance, balance and integrate healthy lifestyles, build powerful relationships, and achieve ultimate well-being. Please, join me in **Leading Under Pressure**.

Gabriela Cora, MD, MBA
Miami, Florida, 2010

15

BURNOUT QUIZ

For each item, note the number that best describes your opinion:

1. I have been stressed out for the past six months.

1. Strongly Disagree	2. Disagree	3. Neutral	4. Agree	5. Strongly Agree

2. I feel my job security is threatened.

1. Strongly Disagree	2. Disagree	3. Neutral	4. Agree	5. Strongly Agree

3. The thought of going to work every day stresses me out.

1. Strongly Disagree	2. Disagree	3. Neutral	4. Agree	5. Strongly Agree

4. I feel highly motivated and have high energy at work.

1. Strongly Disagree	2. Disagree	3. Neutral	4. Agree	5. Strongly Agree

5. I am interested in and excited about my job.

1. Strongly Disagree	2. Disagree	3. Neutral	4. Agree	5. Strongly Agree

6. I have the right level of responsibility at my job and have everything under control.

1. Strongly Disagree	2. Disagree	3. Neutral	4. Agree	5. Strongly Agree

7. I stress on Sunday afternoons, thinking about Monday and the coming week.

1. Strongly Disagree	2. Disagree	3. Neutral	4. Agree	5. Strongly Agree

8. I have become bitter about my job.

1. Strongly Disagree	2. Disagree	3. Neutral	4. Agree	5. Strongly Agree

9. I have become bitter with my boss.

1. Strongly Disagree	2. Disagree	3. Neutral	4. Agree	5. Strongly Agree

10. I have become bitter with the company I work for.

1. Strongly Disagree	2. Disagree	3. Neutral	4. Agree	5. Strongly Agree

11. I get easily annoyed by my coworkers.

1. Strongly Disagree	2. Disagree	3. Neutral	4. Agree	5. Strongly Agree

12. I get easily annoyed with my friends and family when I come back home because of stress at work.

1. Strongly Disagree	2. Disagree	3. Neutral	4. Agree	5. Strongly Agree

13. I have a good relationship with my spouse and children.

1. Strongly Disagree	2. Disagree	3. Neutral	4. Agree	5. Strongly Agree

14. I feel envious of other people who are happy in their work.

1. Strongly Disagree	2. Disagree	3. Neutral	4. Agree	5. Strongly Agree

15. Even though I feel stressed, I strive to do a good job at work.

1. Strongly Disagree	2. Disagree	3. Neutral	4. Agree	5. Strongly Agree

16. I give all my energy to my work and I have no energy left in the evenings and over the weekend.

1. Strongly Disagree	2. Disagree	3. Neutral	4. Agree	5. Strongly Agree

17. I am stressed out all the time.

1. Strongly Disagree	2. Disagree	3. Neutral	4. Agree	5. Strongly Agree

18. I am burnt out.

1. Strongly Disagree	2. Disagree	3. Neutral	4. Agree	5. Strongly Agree

19. I have medical problems because of the excessive stress I experience (tension headaches, anxiety, depression, heart problems, or gastrointestinal problems).

1. Strongly Disagree	2. Disagree	3. Neutral	4. Agree	5. Strongly Agree

20. I have been to the emergency room thinking I was having a heart attack and was told I had a panic attack instead.

1. Strongly Disagree	2. Disagree	3. Neutral	4. Agree	5. Strongly Agree

21. I drink more than two cups of coffee or caffeinated drinks to stay awake at work.

1. Strongly Disagree	2. Disagree	3. Neutral	4. Agree	5. Strongly Agree

22. I have increased my alcohol drinking at night to unwind from a stressful day.

1. Strongly Disagree	2. Disagree	3. Neutral	4. Agree	5. Strongly Agree

23. I take sleeping pills (over-the-counter or prescribed) to sleep at night.

1. Strongly Disagree	2. Disagree	3. Neutral	4. Agree	5. Strongly Agree

24. I must work more than 12 hours every day to get the job done.

1. Strongly Disagree	2. Disagree	3. Neutral	4. Agree	5. Strongly Agree

25. I carry my PDA and respond to company e-mails and important phone calls during vacation.

1. Strongly Disagree	2. Disagree	3. Neutral	4. Agree	5. Strongly Agree

Check your results at *www.executivehealth.com*.

INTRODUCTION

THE 12 MOST COMMON BELIEFS THAT WILL BURN YOU OUT

Through my work as a medical doctor, wellness coach, and corporate consultant, I have found the following beliefs to be at the core of the inevitable path to burnout:

12. I need to make $1,000,000 in the next three months to meet my target by the end of the year.

When every challenge and every opportunity is urgent, there is no space to prioritize and plan strategically. If you constantly put out fires, you will have no time to plan your growth. Although there are, indeed, critical times that will demand 100 percent of your full attention, treating every instance as an emergency will drain your energy and burn you out in time.

11. If I work harder, I will produce more.

Although there is a positive correlation between working efficiently and effectively and producing more, as you approach the overwork mark, your accuracy and precision will start to decline. Working harder for a few days when you have a specific project deadline approaching works. Without planning, working harder for extended periods of time without counterbalancing with effective ways to regain your energy and relax will cost you productivity.

10. I will overwork for the next month, and then I will go back to normal.

How many times have you said this? And how many times have you gone back to working fewer hours? The increase of our working hours is inversely correlated with the possibility of cutting down these same working hours. We tend to accommodate to a new work schedule and get used to the new routine. After a few months, we will tend to forget our original plan as we continue to fill our plate with more and more.

9. Yes, triple-book me!

Worried about losing an opportunity or client here or there? Do you say yes to more activities than you can handle only to find yourself out of breath and short of hands? Many fall into this unhealthy habit of agreeing to more situations than they can control, using the "just in case" excuse. Although many successful entrepreneurs occasionally use this strategy, it works best to anticipate the real demand to create a proactive plan of intervention.

8. I have tons of work and I'm the only person who can do my work; I do everything better and faster on my own.

Can you be everywhere at all times? We know. No one works as hard, efficiently, or productively as you do. As you take on more responsibilities and do more, how will you handle your previous activities? If you feel as though you are working 24/7, you will only succeed if you can ask for help. Although you may be an outstanding independent contributor, those who take the time to create highly functioning teams do best over time. Delegate wisely.

7. I will drink more coffee to have more energy.

You may have always had lots of energy in your 20s and 30s, but now, in your 40s and 50s, you feel the need to boost your energy with coffee as an eye-opener. You used to be fine with one caffeinated drink, but it's now two, three, or more to keep you awake and going throughout the day. Although caffeine heightens focus and attention, it also increases physical tension. Do you feel wired by the end of the day?

6. All I need is a few extra drinks, or over-the-counter or prescribed medications so that I can sleep better.

Wired during the day, how do you disconnect at night? Many people downing coffee during the day feel tense and unable to relax to sleep at night. Although drinking a glass of wine with dinner has its health benefits, increased drinking to relax and taking over-the-counter or prescribed medications is an unhealthy habit. After months or years of drinking at night, many wake up in the middle of the night with rebound anxiety, often experiencing signs and symptoms of a panic attack that can be easily confused with a heart attack (myocardial infarction).

5. I will continue to work from home so I can relax.

Many companies had the brilliant idea of helping their executives work more by supplying them with all the gadgets and equipment available to make them comfortable while continuing their work from home. Busy at work and busy at home, it is no surprise that many of these successful executives experienced medical problems related to this increased work pressure without any time to relax. Many people may feel forced to work longer hours these days (especially working from home), but they will also need to find effective ways to relax both at home as well as at work.

4. I can sleep less and work more hours.

Once you have cut down recreational activities to a minimum and you now want to work longer hours, where will you get the time to do so? By cutting down sleep hours, of course! If you have always done well with five or six hours of sleep, sleeping less may not pose much of a problem. However, if you are used to sleeping eight or nine hours every night, cutting down to five or six hours of sleep will take its toll. Although sustainable for a short period of time, this pattern will further stress you to the point of feeling spacey, uncoordinated, and cranky.

3. I am so busy; I don't have time to eat.

You try to justify the lack of time to eat by having a giant dinner and lie like a lion when going to bed, feeling full, bloated, and disgusted. A one-meal-a-day pattern is not unusual in highly functioning executives and entrepreneurs. While starving themselves during the day, they binge at any opportunity to fill their bodies with junk food, desserts, or refined sugars. This pattern is unsustainable. To replace food as a source of energy, many opt to take expensive vitamins, herbs, or some type of stimulant that will cut down their appetite—caffeine being one of the most common.

2. My work life is perfect; I want to work more... My relationship with my family? Fine... Well, my wife is busy with her life and the kids don't speak to me unless they want something from me...

Most people feel the most important reason for their hard work is the ability to provide for their loved ones. And yet, many busy executives and entrepreneurs feel disconnected from their driving source of energy. This is one of the main reasons that many successful men and women feel lonely, isolated, and unhappy.

And what's the NUMBER-ONE belief that will burn you out?

1. I know I am gaining weight, my blood pressure is high, and my ulcer is acting out. I'm taking more medications, and I can't—I won't—change anything in my lifestyle. I am so busy I can't eat well, sleep, or exercise. But this is the way it is and I can't change it.

You have burnt out by now. Most people who are already experiencing stress-related medical conditions minimize the impact their work style has to do with their current health issues until it's too late. You were working 12-hour days and you are now up to 16. The only way you could increase these working hours was by cutting down on your recreational activities, and isn't exercise a time to play? However, eating well, keeping good sleep hygiene, and exercising regularly contribute to helping us stay in prime physical, mental, and emotional condition. Instead of cutting down on exercise, why not consider working out *more* hours during times of increased activity?

LESSONS LEARNED

Write a list of your top 10 unhealthy work or lifestyle beliefs and habits that are leading you to burnout. As you read **Leading Under Pressure**, mark the potential solutions you can start implementing today as you walk down the path of health, wealth, and well-being.

1. _____
2. _____
3. _____
4. _____
5. _____
6. _____
7. _____
8. _____
9. _____
10. _____

For more information, visit *www.executivehealthwealth.com*, contact us at Wellbeing@ExecutiveHealthWealth.com, and call us at (305) 762-7632.

CHAPTER 1

THE MYTH OF LIFE-WORK BALANCE

" *I had just returned from a U.S.-based business trip and hopped onto my next international flight to join my family. I was flying alone, on my way to a family gathering in South America, sitting in a bucket seat in economy class. A man came to sit next to me.*

He was forcing a smile; he had experienced several problems with his connecting flights and had "ended up" in coach, annoyed he missed his first-class seat on another flight. He was not looking forward to an over-night flight in a less desirable seat. At 5 feet 6 inches, I do not experience leg space problems on most airlines, but at more than 6 feet tall my fellow passenger wasn't happy.

We started chit-chatting and he became slightly more enthusiastic as he described his business: He was a broker and investor, partnering with U.S. and European investors in purchasing land in beautiful Patagonia. I listened carefully as he described his busi-ness activities. He seemed to become even more in-terested when he realized I was quite familiar with the hype as well as knowledgeable of the Southern cone's socio-economic culture.

Then came my turn to share what I did for a living. I immediately perceived a significant shift back to his ini-tial tension when I spoke: "I have two practices: On the one hand, I practice medicine on a part-time basis. I am a psychiatrist, and my area of expertise is mood and anxiety disorders. In my work as a doctor, I was seeing many wealthy business owners and executives. In spite of their piles of gold, there was a deep sense of failure; for them, it was never enough, and many felt unhappy with their lives. Many felt they were working 24/7 and felt like they needed to work even more." I looked at him, inviting him to respond, but he was speechless. I continued: "Most were pumping coffee throughout the course of the day to stay awake, and many were drinking alcohol or taking hypnotics at night to go to bed. Some were already taking prescribed stimulants to work even more hours throughout the day, whereas others were taking stimulants to stay awake a second night a week for extra work. Many regretted missed opportunities to spend quality time with their loved ones. More so, when they had the time with their family and friends, they did not enjoy it. They felt a deep disconnection. They thought how much they missed them when they were not together, yet, when they were together, they wished they were somewhere else, at work. Many were coming to see me burnt out, depleted of energy, and with medical problems such as gastrointestinal problems, neck pain and tension, or migraine headaches. Many had already visited emergency rooms thinking they were having a heart attack when they were having a panic attack instead."

I could see my flight companion turn pale, hypnotized by my story. I continued: "So, I realized the medical premise in our healthcare system did not necessarily address all of these issues at the core, but, instead, the system was attempting to treat the obvious symptoms and not addressing the underlying problems that produced the symptoms. I have been very interested in the medical and business interface for years; I had even decided to further my education by adding an MBA to my medical doctorate degree, and so, this is how The Executive Health & Wealth Institute came to existence. My area of expertise as a consultant is in individual and organizational health and wealth. I assist corporate executives and entrepreneurs as they lead under pressure."

My companion was even paler by now. He asked: "How did you know? I have been experiencing everything you mentioned but thought it was all in my head! I work 24/7, make lots of money, regret the time I don't spend with my young ones, I "live" on coffee during the day, I (shyly) drink at night so I can sleep, and I have also taken sleeping pills…I have had a couple of those dreadful waking-up-in-the-middle-of-the-night-with-chest-pain experiences, dismissed them because I had no time to even go to the hospital. It was a dreadful experience. I thought I was alone….

Allow me to unveil the inexorable truth: Life-work balance is a myth, a tempting fairy tale, an illusion that keeps us going as we are trying to contain our needs and wants into an ideal Zen perfection! Instead, the attempt to find this balance is often confused with finding our core sense of well-being: that opportunity to experience peace and tranquility while living in a hectic world.

Working women and men currently face greater responsibilities than in the past. They have access to higher positions in the workplace, endlessly juggling tasks, and attempting to master productive interactions. At the same time, they face increasing household duties. Whereas some succeed while managing this complex act, others end up dreading the once-wonderful new opportunities. Burnt out, energy depleted, or miserably depressed, some executives and entrepreneurs find themselves working like robots. Unable to enjoy their accumulated wealth, "having it all" yet unable to taste enjoyment, many are incapable of taking pleasure in their hard-earned position and financial stability. It's never enough.

Many of these successful professionals and business owners feel that they are being cheated by the system of success. On the one hand they are giving their jobs the best of their lives—their energy and their passion—and yet they are profoundly ambivalent about being worn out in their personal lives. Many give it all at work and feel deflated when they go home. Instead of sharing a good time with their loved ones, they face a number of responsibilities waiting for them as they arrive, tired from an exhausting day. Instead of revitalizing, connecting with their loved ones, relaxing, and enjoying life as they recharge their batteries for the next day, their time at home is just a continuation of a "busy day at work."

It is because of this increase in demands in the workplace and in the "homeplace" that we are in dire need of integrating new lifestyle strategies to effectively manage our busy work life.

The entrepreneur and the corporate executive perform similar tasks every day while living in constant change. A few are able to sustain quality and top performance in a task that requires constant repetition. In our high-demand reality, moving up or across the corporate ladder is a driving force that most executives face at any given time in their professional careers. With constant change, many executives leave behind basic needs as they are consumed with work. Executives do not have a choice other than to master the art of management and integration demanded by the ever-changing, progressive corporate environment demands.

The best athletes have the biological ability to lower their metabolic needs to baseline levels during between-competition periods. This capability allows them to re-energize and increase their output during the next event, match, or game. Like athletes, corporate executives are likely to exert extraordinary outputs of stamina during their careers. But unlike athletes, executives do not have the luxury of sitting down and relaxing to bring their hyperactive metabolism to a resting state before going into another strenuous phase. Instead, they juggle multiple responsibilities at the same time. Top executives go on to resolve the next task even before they have completed the previous one. Top executives strive to anticipate their next move before there is a tangible need for it. At the same time, executives need to create the temporary illusion of unwinding to bounce back from exhausting work while still in action. To succeed, top executives should use their ability to work on multiple issues at different intensities and at the precise speed that each task requires.

Running a single sprint is a rare occurrence in the life of the globe-trotting corporate warrior. Throughout the course of their complex schedules, executives will most likely need to run two, three, or more sprints, at the same time, and keep going in the corporate marathon. This poses a dilemma. As many feel like they are already at their maximum performance, is there any room for improvement? Is improvement unbounded, or is there a limit to our capabilities? If executives feel as though they have "maxed out," can they lead their teams to achieve a higher goal? If so, what is the turn-key? What is that treasured strategy to enable them to do this, once, twice, and all over again?

As athletes strive to break Olympic records, expert physiologists wonder how much longer records will be broken without the "assistance" of stimulants and artificial performance enhancers. Year after year, athletes come closer to and even surpass prior unbelievable achievements. At the same time, athletes and their coaches know how and when to put pressure on to perform at a higher level. Whereas pushing to the next level in a planned way will lead to success, pushing too hard too soon will decrease performance. Likewise, successful executives, professionals, and entrepreneurs need to pay special attention to finding ways to produce more and maximize productivity and performance while striving to be healthy and well.

High-achievers with little tolerance for defeat leave themselves no space to relax before undertaking the next Herculean task. The pressure they put upon themselves to fulfill their dreams and achieve their projects is such that they project their deadlines and write these down on their calendars "To Be Completed: Yesterday." As they succeed, many devote little time to enjoying their accomplishments. Instead, they dive into their next project without savoring their well-deserved victory.

It is this group of executives or entrepreneurs that procrastinates when seeking advice or assistance until it's too late. This group of successful professionals seeks help once signs and symptoms of obvious burnout are present. As these executives realize there is a clear impact upon the quality of their work, they come to a state of disbelief. These high-achievers usually perform at the top level, and their output is that of three or more people instead of one. Nobody around may notice this decrease in performance, but they do. When these outstanding achievers are in their 20s, they are able to push themselves to levels that only a select few have ever reached. As these executives and entrepreneurs grow into their 40s and 50s, their ability to bounce back ceases to be as effective as in the past. What could have gone wrong? As they try over and over again, they realize their unique, praised ability to do it all has left them for good. But, has it?

Some of these successful executives and entrepreneurs increasingly struggle to maintain healthy body weight, cholesterol levels, and blood pressure. They may now find difficulty falling or staying asleep. Or they may experience bodily tension and find it difficult to relax. They may gradually drink more caffeinated drinks during the day to "stay alert and awake," to continue to perform as they did in their 20s. They may have an extra drink at night to fall asleep after an exhausting day. This harmful sequence of events is now in full force, creating a constant negative cycle. Unattended, the risks of this pattern include the potential for illness or disease. The initial symptoms may be vague, such as gastrointestinal complaints, uncontrolled high blood pressure, tension headaches, anxiety, pain, or fatigue. In more extreme cases, these successful executives may end up in the emergency room with chest pain, gastrointestinal ulcers, or full-blown panic attacks. In denial, they may have endured endless doubts about consulting a professional earlier on, in the hopes that this distress would magically disappear. Dreading the stigma of being labeled as sick, anxious, depressed, or physically unfit in any shape or form, they resist any perceived danger of falling from the hard-earned pedestal of invincibility as the super-powered, successful entrepreneur or executive.

In my years of experience working with high-achievers and successful executives, professionals, and entrepreneurs, I have consistently found that it is this group that truly benefits from implementing a comprehensive, proactive, and integrated approach to wellness. Your roadmap to well-being includes:

☑ **Learn how stress affects your health.** The first step is to know the facts:

- ✓ Understand the relationship between stress and well-being.
- ✓ Identify your pressure points.
- ✓ Learn about stress, resilience, depression, and anxiety.
- ✓ Learn about how stress can impact upon your physical health.
- ✓ Learn how to implement a plan to improve your health.

☑ **Assess your health and wealth baseline.** The second step is to assess your individual and organizational health and wealth baseline using the Four Quadrants of Leading Under Pressure (detailed in Chapters 4 and 7) and to align with the corresponding strategies.

☑ **Implement Effective Strategies.** The third step is to implement effective strategies to maximize peak performance and productivity while also maximizing health and well-being.

If you are **Leading Under Pressure**, it will be a question of time to decide when you are ready to take the driver's seat. Today is a great day to start: assess, fix, and plan ahead. As an executive or entrepreneur, you have dedicated a great part of your life to your career or business. With **Leading Under Pressure** you will address the first step of your journey. My next book, *Managing Work in Life* (*www.managingworkinlife.com*) will go a step further in providing more tips and strategies to maximize a healthy lifestyle. Let's get started by providing the key elements to create your own **New Life Business Plan**—an interactive program I've created that will allow you to assess your current situation and track your progress as you effectively integrate work in life (*www.newlifebusinessplan.com*). Integrate your plan as you merge analyses and strategies into a comprehensive mode of action. Combine individual, professional, and organizational needs and wants in an effective, integrative, and long-lasting plan. *Quantum Wellbeing* (*www.quantumwellbeing.com*) is the culmination of the series of books and audiovisual resources with the broad implementation of healthy lifestyle strategies in your daily routine, putting it all together, practicing and mastering each and every dimension to the fullest.

THE IDEAL WORLD: THE RULE OF THIRDS

If we lived in an ideal world, we would abide by the rule of thirds. First, we would work or study eight hours of the day. These would be our "productive" hours, which would allow us to support ourselves or learn the skills to eventually become self-sufficient. Next, we would spend eight hours in recreational activities: exercising, participating in sports, enjoying the arts, reading for fun, playing, and actively interacting with our friends and family. Last, but not least, in the ideal world, we would recover our energy by sleeping eight hours every night, refreshing our bodies and minds to start a new day with plenty of energy and stamina.

How many of you live in this ideal world?

Our life demands start as young children: much of our day is spent away in daycare centers or school. A stay-at-home parent caring for her child has her—or his—demands too. As children enter the school system, further challenges arise as they are required to pay more intellectual attention in class with less recreational breaks. As the child is now progressively independent, the school workload increases: the adolescent is coached and prepped for college. Ten-year-olds are expected to work on their homework for several hours when they arrive home, and their parents, many of whom have been at work all day, become grumpy watchdogs to ensure the assignments are complete. Teachers are pressured to ex-

Figure 1: The Ideal World

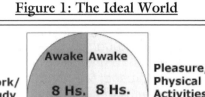

pect young boys and girls to sit still for hours at a time. There is little tolerance but for the quiet, calm, obedient, and attentive: the "perfect" child. Participating in competitive sports adds to the mix, and then, as young adults go to college or join the workforce, additional challenges fall on their plate.

Living in the ideal world is far from tangible reality. Instead, people work an average of eight-plus hours, sometimes reaching 12-, 14-, and 16-hour days, to continue to produce the same as they were producing in previous years.

THE REAL WORLD: THE ARE NO RULES

"I have been dealing with depression, anxiety, and attention problems all my life," the powerful business owner said during our first meeting. "I start my day before the sun rises; I work all day but need to work some more when I come home. I'm here because I need to close some very important deals over the next three months. Forget about enjoying myself, I don't have any time or energy for myself or for my family. I need to have this energy back so that I can work 16-hour days. Dr. Amphy has already prescribed stimulants for me but they are not working as well as they used

35

to; I think I need a higher dose. I have no energy whatsoever."

"I disagree," I said, with caution but assertively, even though these were my first words with this powerful businessman whose previous doctor was a well-respected expert and colleague. "Based on everything you have been doing, my sense is you have tons of energy. You seem to use it all at work, though. The real issue will be to plan how to better distribute your energy throughout your day, so that you can perform and produce at your best during your time at work, and so that you can have a great time with your family and loved ones. That's all...."

That *is* all.

We have an easier time knowing *what* we need to do rather than *how* to do it.

Do you feel it's you I'm talking about? You are not alone. As our workload and responsibilities increase and we start working more hours, we can only make more time by discarding recreational time, gradually knocking this "free" time to a minimum. On a practical level, our work time may increase to the point that there are few moments to share with our friends and loved ones, and less so with ourselves. It is not uncommon for people to reduce their exercise or meal time in order to work more! We now work 12- to 16-hour days, with virtually no time for other activities. At the same time, this "free" time is not necessarily "free," as it is during this time that we will run errands, go to the doctor, or take care of family matters.

Is there any way we can "create" time in our busy schedules?

The only way we can add to our waking cycle is, of course, to stay awake longer hours. The next step to stay awake and work even more is to further cut down our sleep hours by one, two, or three hours, sometimes sleeping less than five hours every night.

Some people have always slept five hours every night and have always felt refreshed during the day. Yet, others who need seven or eight hours of sleep won't succeed in the long run when sleeping fewer hours. Even those of us who have trained ourselves to stay awake for extended periods of time will need to restore our energy in some way, at some time. Traditionally, training physicians worked long hours in the day and night, sometimes working 100 or more hours every week. Even medicine, though, has looked into its practice and has enforced new rules for residents in training to work no longer than 24-hour-shifts at a time. This decision is in clear contrast to prior training times in which residents worked for 36-hour-plus shifts, with no sleep, for years! Some of the reasons behind changing these work schedules relate to an honest attempt to decrease the incidence of accidents or mistakes while at work. In addition, many residents who were driving home at odd hours after working for two days straight had more driving accidents. Others made mistakes they could have avoided had their minds and bodies been well-rested. The issue at stake is: can we truly and effectively sustain "perfect" attention, concentration, and physical response times after extenuating days? The simple answer is: NO!

Some of us may have an easier time bouncing back, based on our constitutional buildup, our genetic predisposition, and the environmental setting. Some of us can certainly do this easily for brief periods of time. Some others struggle even with one night of staying awake, and it may take them longer to recover and go back to a normal schedule. Many successful executives and business owners resort to resting during vacation. Although vacation time is excellent for refueling our energy by eating at structured times, sleeping well, and enjoying recreational activities, the "on at work, off on vacation" is not the healthiest of strategies. Instead, it may be best to create on mini-vacations regularly.

Figure 2: The Real World

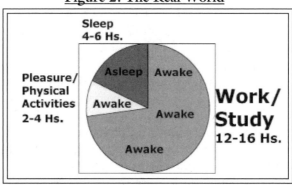

THE WELL-BEING & STRESS CONTINUA

Many successful executives and entrepreneurs tend to work more during hard times. Let's say they have been working 12-hour days and they are now working 16-hour days. The only way they may have been able to do this is by cutting down on recreational activities. A common excuse for reducing exercise time or discontinuing it altogether is feeling the pressure to work more. Exercise is one of the best sources of physical stamina, and by ceasing to do it, this person who's hard at work has lost his or her main fountain of energy. Stress then starts creeping up as one of the most effective biological mechanisms we have to control it fades away.

Stress can be an inspiring source of energy, motivation, and inspiration. However, if stress increases and our way to counter-balance escalating demands falls short, our system gives in with burnout, exhaustion, and disease.

The well-being and stress continua concept provides for a practical way to assess our degree of well-being. To my surprise, I have been encountering more and more people telling me that the culprit for all their aches and pains is the enormous amount of stress they endure. Whereas stress may be the trigger, many are experiencing obvious signs and symptoms of illness and disease at a stage when stress can just aggravate the situation—but it is not the cause.

The stigma of being ill has played a major role in entrepreneurs' and executives' habit of ignoring their underlying physical ailments, which include significant degrees of heart, gastrointestinal, neurological, depression, and anxiety problems. Telling the world they are extremely busy and stressed is expected; after all, they are "supposed" to be working incredibly long hours and competing at their top level. Instead of seeking help in a timely fashion, many are daring to visit their physicians only *after* they have started to experience more than one medical problem.

Busy executives and entrepreneurs may face a crisis that acutely increases their stress level, they may encounter chronic stressors on a regular basis, or they may experience a combination of both. This is why it is of essence that they learn to use stress as a positive source of energy. Although they need to fix their current problem, once it is resolved, they should continue to improve their overall situation. But when stressed out, company executives and entrepreneurs stay at the "firefighter" stance, fixing what is broken, and out of stamina to seek for further growth. If operating in this mode, many attempt to go back to the previous situation and find that status quo, in a futile attempt to avoid inevitable change. The corporate warrior will strive to resolve the challenge at hand and spin the situation as an opportunity to continue to improve and advance to a new level. An unforeseen critical or traumatic event or a series of events may increase stress levels that may acutely affect the person's continuous improvement to maximize well-being. This has been a characteristic of the current recession, wherein levels of pressure have been increasing and unremitting. A helpful analogy may be to compare one critical event to being struck by lightning once—and surviving—versus being rolled over by giant waves again and again as you can't distinguish the bottom of the sea from the light of day.

Modern Western medicine looks at medical problems with an attempt to fix what's wrong, but it falls short of prescribing health and wellness. For instance, if a healthy individual has a bout of illness such as an infection, the right strategy may be to resolve the infection and to move on. On the other end, if someone's baseline is unhealthy (for example, if he or she is immune-compromised) and this person falls ill, the health strategy should instead focus on resolving the acute issue (the infection) and attempting to reach a healthier baseline, rather than "patching" the situation (improve the immune system). Our culture craves quick fixes and immediate gratification rather than thoughtful planning and comprehensive interventions. With the cloning of health-related Websites, most are inundated with information without the brokers' knowledge to discern between qualified information and promotional advertising shoving vitamins and herbs down your throat. Drinking water is good, and yet drinking too much water may kill you. The wellness industry has exploded with untrained individuals selling anything from magnets to liquids to products to a hungry, eager, and prosperous audience. Doctors who went into medicine to promote health and treat when ill are now reimbursed only for fixing what is wrong in just a few minutes. Instead, many dollars are going to third parties offering services to assist employees in doing their preventive work outside of the trained healthcare industry.

Companies able to integrate health and wellness strategies within the organization will find amazing results in the years to come as their workforce will be at its physical best while optimizing performance and productivity.

The well-being and stress continua are inversely related: the higher the level of stress, the lesser the degree of well-being. While someone can be under stress, he or she may still experience well-being. As pressure increases, the person may still be able to experience wellness, but too much pressure will lead to a point of no return. At that point, compensatory systems start giving in and the energy system becomes exhausted. Each of us has an individual perception of stress; we interpret and respond to stressors in different ways.

Figure 3: The Well-being & Stress Continua

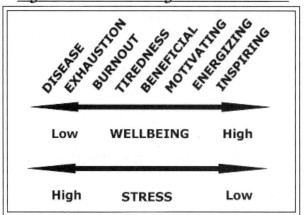

LESSONS LEARNED FROM THE REAL WORLD

1. Life-Work balance is a myth. Instead, seek for an inner feeling of peace, balance, and tranquility.

2. Create your own pie chart: How many hours do you work, have recreational activities, and sleep?

3. Populate each section with all your activities. Start with travel: work at your office, travel time to see clients, flight time, study time, networking, marketing and promotional activities, and so on.

4. Populate your recreational section and include exercise, sports, watching TV, reading for fun, watching movies, vacation, and so on.

5. Sleep: Write all the activities you relate to your sleep time. Include your sleep routine (reading, watching TV, sex, and actual sleep time).

6. Create your past month's calendar and write everything you did in the past month.

7. Create your current activity calendar and write everything you are doing as you go, hourly, daily, and weekly, for the coming month.

8. Check a month later. Are there any differences in your projection?

9. Assess your individual level of stress and well-being in the stress and well-being continua.

10. Write all your current activities in a mind map mode. It should look something like this:

Figure 4: Time & Activity Distribution

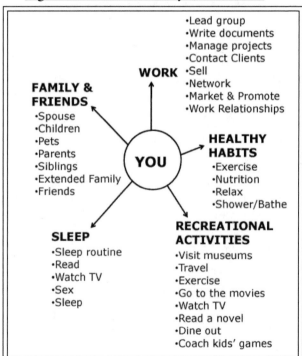

PRESSURE POINTS

These are seven of the self-imposed stressful factors that I most commonly see in my practices:

1. Responding to everything as if it were an emergency; opportunities and challenges are considered immediate priorities.

2. Living up to others' expectations instead of setting your own. You feel as though you are in the middle of several tugs of war, being pulled from each and every direction.

3. Feeling constantly dissatisfied—nothing is enough. You've received your expected promotion, you bought the latest car model, you vacationed at the most exotic resort, and you've sent your kids to the best schools, but, once you achieve your goals, you don't savor the pleasure of your accomplishment.

4. Constantly comparing and competing with others rather than competing with yourself or minding your own business. You want your colleague's office, you want your boss's job, you desire your partner's spouse, and your friends' children are always outdoing yours.

5. Creating impossible deadlines that cannot be achieved by the desired time. You want to make a million dollars in three months, but you made 700,000 in 12 months last year.

6. Stating that one thing is very important but doing something else that does not align with this premise; verbal statements are a mismatch with actions or behaviors. You say you are very concerned about the state of your marriage and your spouse says you don't spend enough time with her. Although you say you want to save your marriage, you go off on a business trip for a month, stating you will take care of your relationship when you return.

7. Moving on to the next level to achieve more without taking a minute to enjoy the present success. You have been blessed with success and yet have a feeling of emptiness

43

and lack. You start working on your next project without enjoying a minute of glory.

What Is Stress?

Most definitions of stress explain it as a focus on environmental conditions that threaten to impair the well-being of the individual. Stress may occur either as an acute event (a one-time event, as in being struck by lightning in my previous example) or as chronic difficulty. It can include a major life event or a small series of events with cumulative effects (either added or multiplied). Although going to college or starting a job are normal age-related expectations, they can still be experienced as stressful to the individual. An extraordinary event such as being abused or imprisoned may also be extremely stressful regardless of whether the person's actions caused the event to occur. The subjective threat of a stressor directly relates to the person's sensitivity toward an event as stressful, and this perception will, in turn, impact the person's psychological well-being. There may be a high genetic predisposition to how each individual perceives and reacts to a stressful situation. Furthermore, some will be able to face some stressors without difficulty (such as stressors at work), and the same person may have a harder time when encountering other stressors (for example, stressors as they relate to their strained relationships with family members). Finally, some specific stressors may be more highly related to depression and anxiety disorders than others.

There is scientific evidence to suggest that a stressor may have a direct effect on the development of a first depressive episode, but not on subsequent ones. This means that someone with a strong predisposition to experience the consequences of sustained levels of stress may develop a first episode of depression during or after the significant stressful event. Eventually, the person may become depressed again, and, although people will try to justify the second episode and link it to another stressful event, there is little evidence to support this. On the contrary, by tracking the series of events in a time sequence, we can identify that the person may have gradually become more depressed and may have started to experience problems with his or her significant other or at work long before the full-blown depression was identified.

Stress *can* be motivating, stimulating, inspiring, and an amazing source of energy. Given the subjective nature of the experience of stress, some of us will thrive under pressure whereas others will succumb to its powerful force. Some executives and entrepreneurs will wait to the last minute to submit proposals, finalize deals, negotiate opportunities, and execute plans, taking advantage of the biological adrenaline rush. Others will pace themselves to find a good balance while timing easier tasks with more complex ones. People's reaction to stress is very different.

Although the most stressful life events include the death of a spouse, divorce, lack of freedom, the loss of a job, or the death of a loved one, stressful events don't necessarily need to be negative in nature. These, though, can be a tremendous source of stress. Becoming a parent may be a wonderful *and* stressful experience. I have particularly seen this in businesswomen who have their first child in their late 30s or early 40s. Many continue strenuous exercise until their personal physician asks them to stop playing tennis, flying, or lifting heavy boxes during their eighth month of pregnancy. Many feel that they will go back to their full workload immediately after delivering their child. They soon find themselves in the dilemma of wanting to spend more time with their baby and having a highly demanding job. Pregnancy and parenting add an important source of stress both from an emotional as well as physical perspective.

Pressure Points

☑ **Physical pressure points:**
  ✓ Fatigue and being overly tired.
  ✓ Physical exhaustion.
  ✓ Sleep deprivation.
  ✓ Having no time to eat.
  ✓ Overexercising.

45

☑ **Emotional pressure points:**

- ✓ Conflict with spouse and children.
- ✓ Conflict with parents and siblings.
- ✓ Conflict with friends.
- ✓ Conflict with boss, colleagues, employees, or clients.

☑ **Intellectual pressure points:**

- ✓ Inability to keep up with work demands.
- ✓ Lack of time to study or prepare.
- ✓ Intellectual exhaustion secondary to sleep deprivation.

☑ **Social pressure points:**

- ✓ Isolation.
- ✓ Lack of connectivity with others at home or at work.
- ✓ Social mismatch between family of origin, friends, and/or work.

☑ **Spiritual pressure points:**

- ✓ Disconnect between personal and organizational values.
- ✓ Feeling that you don't fit in with family of origin or at work.
- ✓ Lack of alignment between life expectations and reality.
- ✓ Feeling that there is no reward after so much effort.
- ✓ Inability to experience a deep spiritual connection with higher being.

LESSONS LEARNED

Write a list of your top 10 pressure points. As you read this book, mark the potential solutions you can start implementing today as you walk down the path of health, wealth, and well-being.

1 _____

2 _____

3 _____

4 _____

5 _____

6 _____

7 _____

8 _____

9 _____

10 _____

ACUTE AND CHRONIC STRESS

Acute stress may cause a series of signs and symptoms ranging from mild anxiety to an acute panic attack or a freezing reaction. However, prolonged, unrelieved exposure to a variety of stressors may cause a person to operate in a physiological "full-alert" or emergency mode at all times, as if a catastrophe was about to occur at any moment.

Whether the outside stressor continues to exist or whether the person fails to return to his or her baseline level of functioning, it is essential for the person to create a state of mind of control. If the person continues to experience a stressor as constant, whether or not the stressor is actually present in the environment, the person runs the risk of failing to adapt to the same stressor through time, potentially exhausting the ability to bounce back and master the situation. If fatigue occurs, the capability of the individual's system to refuel itself gives in, potentially repeating the same errors over and over again. This is why many continue to operate under stress mode even if the stressor has disappeared: they do this because they are exhausted and unable to refresh their systems. An easy analogy is when we overwork our computer and it freezes. There's nothing we can do except to reboot it. Instead, we can avoid this by opening fewer applications at a time, saving our work as we go, and taking more time to work in each program.

47

Whereas stress affects all dimensions of the human being, what may generate a challenge within one area will further impact upon other dimensions if left untreated. For instance, if I am disorganized at work, only my schedule may be impacted upon at first, but, eventually, my disorganization will impact each and every area of my life: I will be double or triple booked, I will miss appointments, I will not complete my work, I will fail to execute on a high level, and so on. On the individual side, if I have untreated high blood pressure, I will eventually suffer from multiple system problems: I will experience headaches, heart problems, kidney problems, or fatigue and anxiety, to name a few. Sustained elevated levels of stress hormones may potentially impair memory with time. High cortisol levels may promote loss of nerve cells, further producing atrophy of key brain structures that may affect future responses to stress. Neuroplasticity (the brain's ability to reorganize itself by forming more neural connections through life) becomes a key element for remastering and retraining ourselves to respond more positively to acute or chronic stress, thus modifying our chances of mastering long-term difficulties.

LESSONS LEARNED

Write your top five acute stressors.

1 _____

2 _____

3 _____

4 _____

5 _____

Figure 5: Acute and Chronic Stress

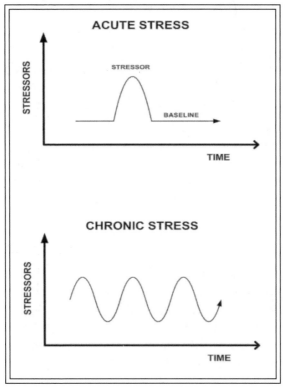

Chronic stress relates to continuous stress. Although not described in psychiatry, many people may be subjected to ongoing, constant stress rather than being exposed to an acute or a single traumatic event. This could better be described as a **Constant Traumatic Stress syndrome,** whereby the person is exposed to both acute events and constant stressors of different magnitudes. An example of this is people living in countries at war, both as civilians or as military personnel. Also, those operating under extreme circumstances where there is ongoing violence while business is "operating as usual" may be subjected to chronic stress.

We need more medical and psychiatric studies to find the differences in the physiology of people exposed to a single traumatic event versus people enduring ongoing trauma and their responses to master this stress.

Corporate executives and entrepreneurs face both acute and chronic stress on a regular basis: acute instances of stress (for example, a specific deadline such as the opening of a new facility or the launch of a new product) as well as ongoing, "chronic" levels of stress (for example, the third downsizing in three years). An example of both is executives in charge of an operation in countries with increased ongoing violence facing individual security problems on a regular basis. Our recent experience through the recession exemplifies chronic stress—although many initially thought the recession was going to come and go as a single episode, we later realized the pressure continued to increase and was unremitting over time.

Types of Chronic Stress

- ☑ **Periodic Stressors** are similar stressors that occur on a regular basis, such as submitting monthly reports.

- ☑ **Occasional Stressors** are unanticipated stressors of differing magnitude. The person may go back to baseline between stressors. An example is dealing with an unhappy client or having trouble with an important delivery.

- ☑ **Cumulative Stressors** are unanticipated stressors of differing magnitude that do not allow the person to go back to baseline and recover. The best example is the global financial recession.

Entrepreneurs and executives most commonly experience multiple stressors of different magnitude at the same time and at different times.

LESSONS LEARNED

Write your top five chronic stressors.

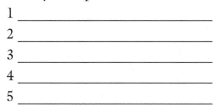

1 _____

2 _____

3 _____

4 _____

5 _____

Figure 6: Types of Chronic Stress

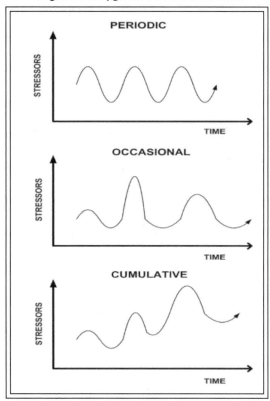

THE STRESS RESPONSE AND RESILIENCE

As described earlier, stress relates to the absolute magnitude of the stressor and the person's perception of the stressor. The fight-or-flight-or-freeze response interferes with high-level intellectual functioning and basically affects each and every dimension. The "sink or swim" analogy also falls in this category.

Unattended, longer-term effects of stress include problems at work, in school, or at home. Stress impacts upon significant relationships with spouses, children, family members, friends, and colleagues.

Signs of Stress Across Dimensions

☑ **Physical signs of stress:**
- ✓ Fatigue.
- ✓ Dizziness.
- ✓ Headaches.
- ✓ Sweating.
- ✓ Gastrointestinal problems.
- ✓ Heart palpitations.
- ✓ Hyperactive startle reflex.
- ✓ Tremors.
- ✓ Colds.
- ✓ Vague pains and aches.
- ✓ Change in sleep pattern.
- ✓ Change in diet.

☑ **Emotional signs of stress:**
- ✓ Fear.
- ✓ Terror.
- ✓ Anger.
- ✓ Guilt.
- ✓ Anxiety.
- ✓ Depression.

✓ Frequent crying.

✓ Irritability.

✓ Inappropriate humor.

✓ Decreased interest in pleasurable activities.

✓ Emotional exhaustion or feeling overwhelmed.

✓ Helplessness.

✓ Hopelessness.

✓ Emotional outbursts.

☑ **Intellectual signs of stress:**

✓ Reduced attention.

✓ Decreased concentration.

✓ Calculation difficulties.

✓ Memory problems.

✓ Decision-making difficulties.

✓ Confusion.

☑ **Social signs of stress:**

✓ Social withdrawal.

✓ Isolation.

✓ Increased substance use to "relax and relate."

✓ Being more vulnerable to peer pressure.

☑ **Spiritual signs of stress:**

✓ Questioning values and beliefs.

✓ Constant cynicism.

✓ Loss of meaning or purpose.

✓ Directing anger toward God.

What Is Resilience?

Resilience is the ability to positively adapt in the face of adversity. Our perception of stressful factors and our tool box to respond to extreme sources of distress will be key components of our ability to bounce back. People commonly demonstrate different levels of resilience. Our resilience is a combination of our own genetic background, our environmental exposure to different challenges, and our learned behavior to respond. The following are some strategies to build resilience, which is an active process that you may enhance. Please note most people strive to go back to their "normal" baseline after facing challenges—the reality that once existed no longer exists, though. You may want to create the illusion that you have gone back to baseline when, in fact, bouncing back may provide for an excellent opportunity for growth, and moving on to the next phase.

The brain circuitry that "controls" our ability to bounce back includes brain areas such as the prefrontal cortex and the dorsal raphe nucleus in the brainstem. Every time we succeed when coping effectively with a difficult situation, we are priming ourselves to succeed in subsequent stressful situations. In other words, the more we succeed today the better the chances we will succeed tomorrow. When we thrive in tough situations our confidence and resilient system is ready to thrive again. If we fail the first time, many will not give it their best the second time, or they may even give up before a fair try. One thing leads to another; this is why it is so important to enable positive experiences as early as possible so as to continue to have positive experiences. This concept justifies allowing ourselves to savor and experience success in the here and now before moving ahead to the next challenge. Positive work experiences create more positive work experiences. Another common example is public speaking. If we leave the stage in a full-blown panic attack we will tend to have more anticipatory anxiety if exposed to a similar situation in the future. In contrast, if we deliver the talk in spite of the initial tension, we will set up our own "state of mind" to perform well the next time.

Resilience is an area that also relates to our ability to live up to the occasion in a critical situation. There are no tests or surveys that measure who will be able to successfully react to a stressful situation in contrast with someone who will freeze. Someone who may have been trained for extreme situations may become paralyzed during an acute event whereas someone who seems to panic with small, everyday-life issues may be able to play it cool and take charge in a catastrophic-like event.

LESSONS LEARNED FROM CHAPTER I

1. **Life-work balance is a myth.** Instead, find your core and develop a sense of peace and tranquility in a hectic world.

2. **Run the marathon *and* be ready to run several sprints.** As a successful executive or entrepreneur, raise your metabolic level to a marathon-like state: You are always moving, creating, leading, managing, resolving constant challenges, and identifying potential opportunities. When crisis strikes, your best strategy is to be in prime shape on a regular basis.

3. **Learn how stress affects your physical, intellectual, emotional, social, and spiritual health.** Understand early signs of burnout and implement effective strategies as soon as possible to counteract more severe consequences.

4. **Realize how you distribute your time throughout the day.** How many hours do you work, play, and sleep?

5. **Know where you would rate yourself in the stress and well-being continua.** Mark your baseline point and track it over time.

6. **Know your pressure points.** Write them down and mark your strategies to master them.

7. **Identify your current acute and chronic stressors.** Write your top five acute and chronic stressors. Control your chronic stressors as much as possible. This will free your time to be able to face acute and unanticipated challenges.

8. **Identify your most common physical, emotional, intellectual, social, or spiritual symptoms when you are under intense pressure.**

9. **Look back in time and identify how well you responded during stressful times.** If you are working with a team, analyze how others responded during stressful times and identify their talents. Consider organizing and planning a group of interventions with pre-assigned tasks in case of an emergency situation. Role-play, test your plan, and continue to improve the response.

10. **Have a plan to improve your resilience.** Even when we may have a genetic predisposition in the quality of our response to bounce back, most people improve with experience.

Interview 1

"Be Cool"
BRIAN DYSON

Brian Dyson knows too well how being cool daily and in the toughest of negotiations characterizes an outstanding leader. His moment of truth came when he was promoted from president of Coca-Cola South Latin America to president of Coca-Cola USA in 1978—a huge jump up the ladder. At the time, he was both the youngest and the first foreigner to occupy this position, coming into a situation of restructuring relationships, which he successfully carried to fruition.

Early in his position, he discovered that he would need to sink or swim. Survival was the only option. As a franchise business, The Coca-Cola system in North America had a fixed price contract dated back to a 1921 legal settlement. Before he came to the United States, the CEO of the company had decided to address this issue by issuing a new contract that all franchisees were expected to sign. The tough sell was having franchisees sign a new contract that did not seem to be in their best interests. Dyson was assured that the new contract amendment discussions would be successfully agreed upon prior to his arrival. The truth is, they were not.

Dyson had been placed, unwittingly, in an untenable position. To fail would mean the end of his career, and in a very public way, given the stature of Coca-Cola. He credits his survival to a quick assessment of his predicament and his plan to counter the odds against him. It took him 18 months to turn the corner. Throughout his ordeal, he maintained an almost humorous approach to his Herculean quest: if things didn't work out, he could always go back to his ranch in Argentina.

Dyson went on to become president of Coca-Cola North America, and he later became president and CEO of Coca-Cola

57

Enterprises in 1986. His lifespan at Coca-Cola comprised 35 years once he retired in 1993.

BRIAN DYSON ON LEADING UNDER PRESSURE

With scholarly precision, Mr. Dyson was generous with his time and his sharing of his pearls of wisdom. He wanted to ensure the accuracy of our discussion. I couldn't but ponder how this personal characteristic would prevail in his work.

Dyson: As a prologue to this discussion I believe that feeling pressure is far more pervasive than we realize. You may be in charge of a major public company and be subjected to the pressure of "enhancing shareholder value," but your spouse may feel similar pressure to prepare your children for life. So we all need to understand this reality.

Any time you wish to achieve something, in any walk of life and whatever your position, you will be pressed. As the expression goes, "the fleas come with the dog." Though being the head of a large international corporation is a visible example of leading under pressure, the same nerve-wracking feeling will be visited on an entrepreneur struggling to make payroll.

Cora: *Was your perception of the pressure you endured early on when leading smaller groups similar to what you experienced later in your career?*

Yes. When you start out, the stakes may be much lower for the corporation, but for you, it is everything—you have no safety net and very little seasoning.

Effective leaders seem to combine their knowledge with their experience and a touch of intuition. What are your thoughts?

Absolutely. On any particular issue, the first thing is to fully understand it—to know it from all perspectives. Experience will help you decide how to handle it and when: Is it a "now" issue, or can you let it simmer, mature, and, hopefully, cool down? And intuition is pervasive in all this process: like, does your intended action feel right?

Do you feel you had a particularly unique ability to juggle multiple challenges? Is there anything else that you implemented as you experienced increasing pressure?

Yes, I was always able to multitask, to juggle more balls than normal, but I also grew my ability to do this. The danger is to become overloaded—to be beaten down by the pressure of [having] too much on your plate.

Here's what I did. The first rule is equanimity; to keep your cool. How? Try a little perspective. You're not exactly facing famine, or flood, or frontline, life-or-death situations. In fact, you are alive and well, living free and looking to, say, a round of golf on the weekend. So let's recognize that your issues are quite manageable and not life-threatening—which they might become if you let stress get the better of you. So lighten up and be happy.

Then you must learn to focus. Take each issue in order of importance and urgency, and then give it its due in terms of clean, clear thought. If necessary, write down your conclusions and then go to the next. And if these same issues tend to interrupt your sleep, try to develop the discipline to say, "No way. I've already thought them through. There's nothing to add. Ciao. Sayonara. Goodbye." I know, it's easier said than done, but lying awake is worse.

One final suggestion: Learn to delegate. When [it's] done properly, you'll be able to juggle 20 balls instead of 10.

You are raising some very significant points here. First, you are sharing with me about how to put things in perspective by comparison. You are making decisions about what comes first, second, or third as you prioritize. Next, you are talking about your ability to resolve challenges in your mind. You are identifying all possible challenges and proactively thinking about how to improve and resolve them, achieving a positive solution. You are also addressing your discipline in learning to delegate. Have you found anything else that has helped you and your colleagues to stay well while continuing to do an excellent job?

There are, for me, two other disciplines tha are perhaps the most important: One is fitness; the other is maintaining balance in your life.

Fitness first. You'd think it is obvious; even the ancient Romans proclaimed *mens sana in corpore sano*—"a sound mind, in a sound body," right? Yet why is it the first discipline to go when under pressure? Me, I go the other way: the more pressure I feel, the more I need to exercise. Just get up and go for a walk—you'll feel better, and make better decisions.

I can recall many meetings in which I felt the tide was running against me, or where some financial nerd was deliberately trying to baffle me with numbers, or there was obfuscating legal mumbo-jumbo…what do you do? Try looking across the table at your tormentor and [saying to] yourself, "I bet he can't do an Olympic-length triathlon. Or boot camp at 5 a.m." You'll immediately feel better and be back in control of your own agenda.

Finally, you must maintain balance in your life—family and friends, body and soul. If you lose your balance with any of these, you will be in far more trouble than any work-pressures may bring. Keep your balance and you will do just fine.

———

Indeed he has. **Brian Dyson** was a pioneer of staying in good balance and wellness before people would talk about juggling multiple tasks or finding healthy ways to stay on top of your game. He retired from the Coca-Cola system in 1994, but remained active as a consultant to the company. In August of 2001 he came out of retirement and accepted the position of vice chairman and chief operating officer of The Coca-Cola Company. Mr. Dyson is currently president of Chatham International

Corporation (CIC), a private international business consulting and investment firm with emphasis in South America. As such, he remains active in projects relating to his investments and is on the board of various companies. He earned his BA from Facultad de Ciencias Economicas in Buenos Aires and later attended Harvard Business School. He's the author of *Pepper in the Blood* (Chatham International Corporation, 1996).

CHAPTER 2

DO YOU NEED A COACH OR A DOCTOR?

Stress is the buzzword of the 21st century. Even young children come home saying they are stressed out these days. Many companies, executives, and entrepreneurs have hired coaches—many of whom left their own corporate jobs because of burnout—to help increase performance at work. Although efficiency may be helpful in maximizing our ability to produce, coaches may not be as helpful when the person is already synthesizing energy with plenty of coffee during the day and having trouble sleeping at night without the use of alcohol or hypnotics. Many of these successful executives seek to see a doctor when they are already experiencing heartburn, chest pain, or panic attacks.

Instead, I'd like to see people preventing these physical events from even happening. People who are experiencing a series of medical issues (on which the healthcare system is particularly focused) triggered by stress may not benefit from coaching as much as people who are healthy and want to improve their performance at work. Everyone who is leading under pressure needs to prioritize health, implement treatment as necessary, and improve lifestyle strategies.

You will benefit from having a coach if you are performing and producing at a good baseline level and if you want to continue to improve. You will also benefit from a coach if you feel somewhat disorganized and need direction in how to prioritize, plan, or organize your day. Lastly, you will benefit from a coach if you feel the need of an outside force to keep you on track. Questions you should ask include:

- ☑ Am I a good self-starter?
- ☑ Do I need external pressure to perform at a high level?
- ☑ Have I reached my best and need additional help to go to my next level?
- ☑ Am I facing new challenges with little experience?
- ☑ Am I in a new job?

On the other hand, you may benefit from having expert professional assistance if you would like to implement healthy lifestyle strategies while working on improving your performance and productivity, managing work in life, and improving in each and every area of your life.

Executives and entrepreneurs who are constantly leading under pressure can succeed by integrating effective strategies to address both performance and productivity issues while optimizing lifestyle strategies. By integrating both, they can achieve their best while remaining healthy and experiencing well-being. In essence, it's important to intervene with the right approach. A business coach may be very effective in helping you maximize your performance, but you will hopefully visit a cardiologist if you are experiencing heart trouble. In addition, the overwhelming amount of information on the Web creates the illusion of being able to do it yourself. I wouldn't dare fly a commercial plane or operate complex machinery after watching a movie on planes or engineering. Seeking assistance from experts will save entrepreneurs and executives the precious time they don't have to spare to begin with.

PERFORMANCE AND PRODUCTIVITY AT WORK

Cathy is considered a star by her team of teams. She's well-liked, well-respected, and dependable. Although she has always performed on a high level, Cathy has started to notice her subtle decline in meeting deadlines, doing things at the last minute, or even having spelling errors in her e-mails and written work. These things would never have happened to her before. She had always viewed herself as being highly efficient, managing her time effectively, and feeling in control of every aspect of her work. She's been so successful she's had the unusual opportunity to advance faster than her colleagues. She wonders what has been happening lately. She has experienced lots of change at work. Cathy has just received her much-anticipated promotion, but this opportunity came tied with an unanticipated event: Her fellow team just lost its leader and she was asked to take over the other team. She is now leading 20 managers instead of 10, and she doesn't know how long she will be doing this. A "yes" woman, Cathy feels stretched too thin, and, although she has much support from her staff, she's a strong believer that the buck ends with her. Looking back, she feels she may have taken on too much too soon.

Cathy is a well-established leader with an excellent track record. Although her performance and productivity would probably have continued at the top level, she may have juggled too many challenges too soon without having the proper support to do it all. She could have continued to excel, but the unanticipated responsibility of doubling her direct reports threw her off. She can't control the situation. Leaders who operate under pressure effectively set up processes that work like clockwork while being on the watch for unanticipated challenges. Cathy hasn't had the time to do this, but this strategy will help her control her situation as much as possible.

Performance

Performance reflects both an active process (how things get done and how long it takes for them to get done) and the outcome (quality of the product and productivity). As an effective leader, you must operate on two paths simultaneously: the performance path with productivity as the final destination, and the people path, overseeing your employees' health, as described by Dr. Len Sperry in *Effective Leadership*. The full range of health and well-ness includes being observant of the levels of stress in your work-force. Being effective as a leader involves your expertise in all areas—for yourself, for your team, and for your organization. To be consistent, you can't promote life-work balance and demand documents be submitted by midnight. Although you can do this occasionally, you need to be aware of how often the *extraordinary* happens. Effective and efficient leaders will know how to handle the pressures: keeping an eye on what needs to be done in the here and now, with the other eye on the future.

The performance process is a dynamic development. As an active, fluid process, it presents the outstanding opportunity to improve from point A to point Z. As you get started, you want to evaluate your baseline performance so as to set up a goal plan to continue to improve. At work, your performance evaluation includes the examination of the degree of knowledge, skills, abilities, quantity and quality of work, attitude toward work, communica-tion skills with others, level of initiative, degree of cooperation, dependability, judgment, leadership, organization, and planning abilities.

An adequate performance assessment system in business may include several components and should serve the purpose of overall and ultimate improvement. This purpose is fulfilled by having a feedback system in place, and will provide a tool and basis for salary increases and promotion, and overall direction of an employee's work. This opportunity will also enable you to identify specific areas for further training or improvement of skills for additional development.

Productivity

Productivity is a measure of outcomes and is the relationship of input to output. As productivity increases, profits increase, as well as competitiveness in business or market share.

Based on the type of operation you and your business are involved in and what you are producing, you should choose a convenient measure of productivity. Measuring this dimension also includes a time frame in which you measure it.

Productivity will mean something different to each business whether it produces tangible products or intangible services. The standard measurement of productivity is output per worker-hour, or the ratio between the number of hours worked and the total output. You can also measure your productivity per week, month, or year, if each unit of production takes more than an hour to create. Output can be measured in terms of volume, quantity of items produced, and the dollar value of the items produced.

It may be easier to measure your level of productivity if you concentrate, specifically, on your "produced output" at work. Based on our individual skills and capabilities, our training, studies, and experience, many of us may produce a proportional equivalent of the input we have invested. Some produce more and others produce less. For example, if I have had 12 years of education and training for the sake of learning and then decide not to work, or to work in an area completely different from the one in which I trained, some would argue the output produced in another area may not correspond with the input of trained years. On the other hand, if I am able to actively produce in accordance with the amount of invested training, the alignment may be perfect. Aligning the input with the product output is essential as an efficient use of energy.

When we are at our best, focused, well-rested, and relaxed, we may spend—let's say, for the sake of an example—one hour of our time to produce the desired output (service or product). When, instead, we become progressively tired, inattentive, and distracted, what would take an hour when refreshed will now take two or three. Although the quality of the end product may still be high, performance and productivity will not be at their best.

MEDICAL ILLNESSES WITH A
STRESS COMPONENT

Albert is a CEO in his late 50s. He has been a successful family man and leader of a large financial organization for years. For the past decade, he has experienced increasing pressure at work, as more competing companies have come into existence. Many have disappeared while he continued to sail his ship despite the rough seas. His adult children are caring for themselves, yet Albert feels as though he carries a world of responsibilities on his back. Although he intellectually understands his role, he feels responsible for every person within his organization and believes nothing works well unless he is there to handle it all. Albert is a self-made man, trained in the traditional style: A company owner needs to be involved from A to Z. His managers and employees firmly believe he micromanages everyone at work, and he will often call work during family time or vacation (that is, if he takes vacation at all). Albert believes the world will fall apart unless he is everywhere. He has been visiting his family physician more often in recent months. His doctor has told him how stressful events have impacted upon his health, leading to episodes of high blood pressure and gastrointestinal problems. In spite of his doctor's recommendations, Albert stopped exercising after an unanticipated financial loss, feeling he had to dedicate more time to work. He has experienced severe headaches, which were linked to high blood pressure episodes. He has been treating his high blood pressure and headaches with medications. Additionally, he has been experiencing gastrointestinal upset for years, and has been restricting his diet more and more as he has developed food sensitivities. He has difficulty sleeping and feels drained and grumpy most days. His hectic schedule doesn't help: Albert travels coast-to-coast, across meridians, around the globe, adjusting to different time zones, cultures, and nutritional styles.

In this example, Albert has some longstanding patterns that may have offered chronic stress factors, such as constantly micromanaging staff, feeling indispensable, or not taking breaks to relax or exercise. In addition, acute stressors such as his current financial loss may have contributed to additional sources of stress with further impact on his health.

Increasing levels of stress may affect individuals to different degrees. Highly functioning individuals may struggle to organize their activities as well as they used to. A successful executive or entrepreneur who was working at his or her best may experience a significant decline in his or her performance if having marital difficulties or if facing drug problems in their teenage kids. Those who may already be suffering conditions such as diabetes or hypertension may experience worsening of their condition during times of increased stress.

Stress may have a direct impact on each and every system; an overall decline in performance or productivity may become apparent even if the person is present at work. If the vulnerable system is the person's central nervous system, he or she may experience an increase in tension and migraine headaches, a first episode of depression or anxiety, or both. If his or her vulnerable system is the endocrine system, the person's thyroid function may suffer, or worsening of previously stable diabetes may occur. Stress may impact the cardiovascular system by increasing the potential for angina or increasing the probability of having a heart attack. Stress may contribute to triggering an asthma attack, directly impacting upon the pulmonary system, an ulcer via the gastrointestinal system, and so on.

It is essential to understand the differences between stress, depression, and anxiety disorders, as the appropriate intervention for each varies. Unfortunately, many individuals may not recognize their symptoms as signs of an illness, or they may fear the reactions of colleagues, friends, and family. As a result, millions of

69

people with depression or anxiety do not seek treatment. Instead, they experience problems at their jobs and in their relationships that could have been avoided if addressed earlier.

MEDICAL ILLNESSES WITH A STRESS COMPONENT

- ☑ Neurological and psychiatric disorders:
    - ✓ Tension and migraine headaches.
    - ✓ Stroke.
    - ✓ Pain.
    - ✓ Depression.
    - ✓ Anxiety.
    - ✓ Addictions.
- ☑ Endocrine disorders:
    - ✓ Diabetes.
    - ✓ Hypo- or hyperthyroidism.
    - ✓ Adrenal-related conditions.
    - ✓ Early menopause or irregular menses.
    - ✓ Decrease in testosterone levels.
- ☑ Cardiovascular and pulmonary disorders:
    - ✓ Asthma.
    - ✓ Hypertension.
    - ✓ Angina pectoris.
    - ✓ Myocardial infarction.
- ☑ Gastrointestinal disorders:
    - ✓ Colitis.
    - ✓ Gastric ulcers.
    - ✓ Irritable bowel syndrome.

Figure 7: Medical Problems With Stress Component

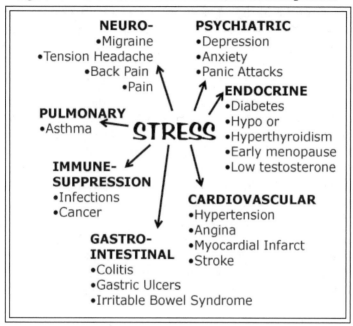

MENTAL HEALTH

In a 2008 survey conducted by the Partnership for Workplace Mental Health and Meritain Health in collaboration:

- ☑ 94% of responders believed their stress level affected job performance.

- ☑ 52% of employees said their employer did not address stress, life-work balance, or mental/behavioral health with employees.

- ☑ 40% of employees said they weren't aware of what mental or behavioral health benefits were offered by their employer.

71

Screening for medical conditions is much more common than screening for mental illness, although mental illness usually accounts for the most indirect cost as compared to other medical conditions, including high blood pressure, diabetes, or back problems. Both absenteeism (missing work) and presenteeism (being present at work but unable to perform or produce because of not feeling well or being preoccupied) are prevalent when people experience depression or other psychiatric conditions.

The costs of depression are high, affecting individuals, their families, and their work organizations. The estimated financial costs of depression in missed days at work, medical expenses, and premature death are $44 billion annually in the United States (Stewart, W.F., et al.: "Cost of Lost Productive Work Time Among U.S. Workers With Depression." *JAMA*, June 18, 2003, pp. 3135–3144).

Individuals with depression are about twice as likely to develop coronary artery disease, twice as likely to have a stroke, and more than four times as likely to die within six months from a myocardial infarction (Sederer, L.I., et al.: "Integrating Care for Medical and Mental Illnesses." *Preventing Chronic Disease*, April 2006).

More so, any chronic medical condition such as back pain, diabetes, headaches, or heart failure with comorbid depression significantly increased cost to the employer per patient, ranging from almost 30 percent to 65 percent as per the National Partnership for Workplace Mental Health.

Depression

Larry has been a successful entrepreneur, caring for his family business for years. In his early 30s, he experienced a period of low energy and lack of motivation, reflected in his apprehension about taking over the family business. Everything seemed to be going well in his business, but he lacked the push to perform at his highest level. His family and friends became worried because he had always been perceived as an overachiever, *enjoying his successes. Larry had always been athletic and always took good care of his health. But now he was unable to sleep well at night, waking up hours before his regular waking time, and unable to go back to sleep. His appetite drastically decreased, and he lost weight, prompting others to alarm. Larry felt the world had lost its beautiful colors and music had lost its harmony. He felt nothing inspired him to continue his daily existence. His wife became increasingly worried when he missed going to work—which was out of character for him—and she consulted his family. Larry's father suggested he visit their family doctor, as he realized that many of the signs and symptoms his son was showing were similar to the ones he had also experienced decades before. Larry had a full work-up and other medical conditions were ruled out. Larry was educated about depression and a successful intervention was implemented. Since then, Larry has effectively dealt with depression. He can identify the early signs and symptoms of depression and intervene as soon as possible.*

Larry's situation is not atypical in someone with a strong family predisposition for clinical or biological depression. Although many would wonder what triggered Larry's depression, a thorough evaluation by a medical doctor would have helped to make the right diagnosis and intervention. This evaluation would rule out the possibility of having other medical conditions impacting upon Larry's mental health. In his case, Larry is already working at a high level. There is a more profound concern about his ability to perform given his medical condition.

Depression is a serious medical illness that negatively affects your thoughts, your feelings, your behavior, your ability to communicate with others, and thus your ability to connect with your loved ones. To receive a diagnosis of clinical depressive disorder, signs and symptoms of depression would be severe enough to impact upon your functioning at work and at home. Depression is a common illness that affects close to 20 million

Americans across gender, age, race, ethnicity, and socioeconomic status every year. Depression most often appears for the first time between the mid-20s to mid-40s. Women experience depression twice as often as men in their lifetime.

Feelings of sadness are expected to arise upon the death of a loved one, the loss of a job, or the ending of a relationship. In the normal process of sadness, feelings of sadness will decrease with time. Instead, clinical depression can continue for months or years if left to its natural course.

Depression includes a variety of symptoms, but a healthcare practitioner will inquire about the presence of a persistent feeling of sadness or the loss of interest or pleasure in usual activities (DSM-IV-TR. *Diagnostic and Statistical Manual of Mental Disorders*, published by the American Psychiatric Association, 2000). Either one or both symptoms must be present for at least two weeks to consider a diagnosis of depression. In addition, the person must experience at least five of the following symptoms: changes in appetite that result in weight loss or weight gain, lack of sleep or oversleeping, loss of energy or increased fatigue, irritability or restlessness, feelings of worthlessness or inappropriate guilt, difficulty concentrating or making decisions, or thoughts of death or suicide or attempts at taking one's life.

Depression is diagnosed only if those symptoms just listed are not due to other medical conditions or are not the unexpected side effects of medications or substance abuse.

If you believe you may have clinical depression, consult your personal physician or a psychiatrist. Depression is one of the most treatable medical conditions, and, with proper treatment, individuals can regain their health and continue to enjoy their lives.

Signs and Symptoms of Depressive Disorders

☑ **Physical signs and symptoms of depression:**
   ✓ Sleep Disturbances—sleeping significantly more or less than usual.

- ✓ Appetite change—eating significantly more or less than usual.
- ✓ Loss of energy.
- ✓ Agitation or slowness.
- ✓ Decreased sexual interest.
- ✓ Physical complaints—vague pains and aches, headaches, or abdominal pain.

☑ **Emotional signs and symptoms of depression:**

- ✓ Anxiety.
- ✓ Nervousness.
- ✓ Lack of pleasure.
- ✓ Melancholia.
- ✓ Depressed or sad mood.
- ✓ Feelings of worthlessness.
- ✓ Irritable or cranky mood; "moody."

☑ **Intellectual signs and symptoms of depression:**

- ✓ Difficulty concentrating.
- ✓ Difficulty focusing.
- ✓ Difficulty completing tasks.
- ✓ Sense of guilt.
- ✓ Low self-esteem.
- ✓ Negative image of self.
- ✓ Disorganized thinking or presence of psychosis.

☑ **Social signs and symptoms of depression:**

- ✓ Social isolation.
- ✓ Withdrawal.
- ✓ Avoidance of interactions.
- ✓ Easily angered or agitated.
- ✓ Change in normal way of interacting with others.

☑ **Spiritual signs and symptoms of depression:**

✓ Loss of interest in daily activities.

✓ Feelings of hopelessness and helplessness.

✓ Suicidal thoughts, acts, or attempts.

✓ Feelings of worthlessness.

✓ Sense of guilt.

✓ Question of values.

✓ Negative outlook of future.

Anxiety

❝ *Alex has always been looked up to and has been considered very successful in all her business endeavors. She has had a recent promotion into a job that is quite demanding, requiring skills she does not feel she has mastered. She experiences daily discomfort, feeling she will be "found out," although her performance and productivity have been excellent. She has always been good at thinking on her feet. She is suddenly asked to give a presentation to upper management without prior preparation. A colleague minimizes the depth the presentation requires and she finds herself in front of unknown people "staring" at her. As she looks around, Alex feels that her heart is about to explode out of her chest, her palms are soaking wet, and she is breathing fast. She blanks her introduction, mumbling shyly and disorganized. The first few minutes are torture but she eventually manages to overcome the unpleasant situation and bounce back. She still does not remember what she was thinking or saying those first few minutes, but the symptoms she experienced are still fresh in her mind and she fears they will come back.* ❞

Alex seems to be in control of her work situation even though she still feels she's learning and not on top of her game after her recent promotion. Increased stress and unusual pressure may have contributed to Alex's first experience of a panic attack. Having one episode does not mean Alex has panic disorder; however, she will still benefit from having a plan in place to avoid any similar situation (as she fears the same event may happen again). If she experiences a second or a third panic attack, and if they subsequently happen in other situations (such as while driving, while driving on a bridge, while on a plane), Alex may have to face this situation with an effective medical approach.

Anticipating a tough business deal, having an important job interview, or giving a presentation to a tough audience may be good reasons for feeling a little anxious. Sweaty palms and "butterflies" in the stomach during challenging situations are not uncommon. However, normal feelings of nervousness differ significantly from anxiety disorders, another very treatable medical condition. An anxiety attack often occurs unexpectedly, impacting upon the daily routine in an unprecedented way. Anxiety disorders are the most common of emotional disorders, annually affecting more than 20 million Americans.

People may try to connect their feelings of nervousness to an event, and these feelings may go away after the event has passed; instead, anxiety disorders often occur for no apparent reason and repeat through time. When anxiety disorders are present, the person reacts as if she or he were in a state of alarm to which the person needs to constantly decide to fight or flee. This exhausting mechanism further burns out the individual, as she or he anticipates the next attack. These alarming reactions can make everyday experiences sources of dread. If left untreated, job performance, work productivity, and personal relationships inevitably suffer as a result.

Much like in depression, anxiety disorders generally respond well to treatment, and the majority of patients receiving treatment experience significant relief from their symptoms. Unfortunately, many people with anxiety disorders do not seek treatment because they do not recognize their symptoms as a sign of illness or they fear the reactions of colleagues, family, or friends. More so, many refer to themselves as being burnt-out, stressed, or exhausted when they are actually experiencing full-blown panic attacks.

Types of Anxiety Disorders

Panic disorder, phobias, obsessive-compulsive disorder, post-traumatic stress disorder, and generalized anxiety disorders are included in this category. I would like to comment on both panic disorders and post-traumatic stress disorders. Busy executives who are leading under pressure need to keep an eye on these two and their potential relationship to the stress and well-being continua.

The key symptom of panic disorder is the panic attack, an overwhelming fear of being in danger or about to die, during which the individual may experience mostly physical, emotional, and intellectual symptoms, including an overwhelming feeling of impending doom with a cluster of symptoms such as pounding heart palpitations, sweating, or shortness of breath, to name a few.

Post-traumatic stress disorder (PTSD) occurs in individuals who have experienced, witnessed, or survived a severe or terrifying event. People with PTSD keep re-experiencing the ordeal 24/7 through memories of the events during waking hours and recurrent nightmares during sleep. They experience flashbacks as well as extreme physical, emotional, intellectual, social, and spiritual distress when exposed to situations that remind them of the traumatic event.

Events that can trigger PTSD include witnessing or experiencing military combat, violent personal attacks, man-made or natural disasters, and physical or sexual abuse.

As in depression, genetic, environmental, and stress factors may contribute to the onset of anxiety disorders.

Signs and Symptoms of Anxiety Disorders

☑ **Physical signs and symptoms of anxiety:**
  ✓ Pounding heart or chest pain.
  ✓ Sweating, trembling, or shaking.
  ✓ Shortness of breath or sensation of choking.
  ✓ Nausea or abdominal pain.

✓ Dizziness or lightheadedness.

✓ Chills or hot flashes.

☑ **Emotional signs and symptoms of anxiety:**

✓ Numbness.

✓ Fear of losing control, "going crazy," or dying.

☑ **Intellectual signs and symptoms of anxiety:**

✓ Feeling of impending doom.

✓ Feeling unreal or disconnected.

☑ **Social signs and symptoms of anxiety:**

✓ Avoidance of frequenting places that "remind" of the event or place where the first episode took place.

✓ Isolation.

☑ **Spiritual signs and symptoms of anxiety:**

✓ Hopelessness.

✓ Fear of death.

✓ Helplessness.

Medical Interventions for Depression and Anxiety Disorders

Consult your personal physician or a psychiatrist if you believe your performance and productivity at work or your interaction with your loved ones are being negatively impacted upon by your experience of depression or anxiety signs or symptoms. Depression and anxiety disorders are two of the most treatable medical conditions, and, with proper treatment, individuals can regain their ability to work at their best, perform at their highest level, and experience significant relationships with their loved ones while experiencing a deep sense of well-being.

With the healthcare shift to offer fewer services to more people while spending less quality time with each individual, general assessments or general screenings or surveys requiring just a few minutes will become more common. Although there is value in addressing general symptoms, nothing beats the face-to-face evaluation by someone who understands the nature of your work, the challenges you face, and the significance of your relationships. An expert professional can help guide you while you rank your priorities, attributing greater or lesser significance to each, all while guiding you to maximize your health and wellness strategies. Whereas many people at different training levels can offer a general triage or screening of your situation, executives and entrepreneurs tend to be a highly educated, up-to-date, information-seeking, and do-it-yourself group. Chances are, by the time you decide to seek help you may have already been experiencing several signs and symptoms of burnout or disease for a long time.

What works best when treating depression or anxiety is to integrate comprehensive and holistic approaches with clear goal-setting strategies. In our fast-paced environment—and with the limited healthcare dollars and time offered to patients—medication management has become the cornerstone of treatment of mental health illnesses. On the other end, by limiting resources, many people end up in unnecessary weekly therapy sessions hoping to modify an underlying biological predisposition that will not be resolved through talk therapy alone. Although psychological interventions can be very effective, there is a time and place for everything. For people experiencing burnout with its physical, emotional, and intellectual consequences of increasing and unremitting levels of stress, integrative approaches are a must—and the best. In contrast with using a "fix it" model, I suggest people fix the situation that got them into trouble, but create a new opportunity to achieve their best while enjoying fulfilling lives. This is a contrast with most of what the current U.S. healthcare system offers in a few minutes of major evaluation or follow-up treatment. Even when providing services as a business coach, I would continue to work on prioritizing strategies and organizational skills, but I would refer my client to have an appropriate evaluation by a family physician or psychiatrist.

The length of treatment or proper combination of interventions is determined on a case-by-case basis, meaning that treatment depends on each individual person. For example, someone experiencing a first mild episode of depression triggered by a catastrophic event with an excellent support system and a healthy history may benefit from being monitored for six months to a year. On the other end, someone experiencing a third episode of severe depression with a strong family history of depression may need to be followed for years.

An effective approach to treating depression and anxiety includes one or a combination of the following interventions.

Psychotherapy

The following psychotherapy styles have been proven effective in the treatment of depression and anxiety disorders: Supportive Therapy, Cognitive-Behavioral Therapy (CBT), Intensive Brief Dynamic Psychotherapy, Interpersonal Therapy, and Psycho-Education. Self-help books may provide a combined educational and CBT perspective. This is the main reason why coaching has become such a hot topic these days. Coaching principles use Cognitive-Behavioral Therapy "light." Although many coaches are trained therapists, the coaching selling point is to avoid going into the *why* and focus on the *how* to set up goals to improve a given situation. This is an effective approach many skilled clinicians use. However, what distinguishes a non-clinician coach from an expert is the expert's ability to help the individual resolve challenges at the core. Experts want to know the source of the problem so that they can help resolve the issue. My preference is to do both. I usually start off by creating a set of useful strategies, and, once they are effectively in place—and working—I'd start discovering and uncovering the underlying issues that created the problem itself. This is a key skill we develop in medicine, as we strive to discover the source of the problem and to avoid just treating a symptom of the problem.

Psychopharmacology

There is increasing apprehension about the use of medication management for psychiatric conditions, and yet, whereas some people should seriously consider managing their anxiety or depression with the proper medications, others should consider adding therapy and lifestyle strategies instead of solely relying on the use of prescribed medications.

The central idea of medication management, or psychopharmacology, relates to helping the person minimize his or her physiologic response to, say a panic attack. The problem with most current treatment practices is the overuse of benzodiazepines, including a favorite, alprazolam (Xanax), followed by lorazepam, clonazepam, or diazepam. Short-acting benzodiazepines such as alprazolam or midazolam end up promoting psychological anticipation of the panic attack and dependency on the medication, causing a vicious cycle of fear and relief. Instead, using antidepressants with anxiolytic properties helps the individual decrease his or her overall level of anticipatory anxiety, preventing a panic attack from even happening, which makes it much easier and tolerable for the person to work on the underlying psychological issues and lifestyle strategies.

Why would you take antibiotics for an infection and hesitate to take medications for a moderate or severe episode of depression?

Many people seem surprised by my positive assessment of medication management. Because I am a wellness coach, many believe I would not use medications and only rely on natural ways of being healthy. Although I am a strong advocate of optimizing lifestyle strategies to promote health and wellness when the person is healthy, I still don't know of any other effective and efficient way to help the person go back to a good level of health and well-being in a timely fashion. Interestingly, many non-physicians sell all kinds of vitamins, herbs, and potions, approved only as food supplements and not approved by the Food and Drug Administration (FDA). Many of these non-physicians are the most critical of prescribing physicians who work with FDA-approved medications, and yet, they sell vitamins and herbs with no proven efficacy! Millions of dollars are spent by people craving a dream potion. Psychopharmacology is an effective biological treatment for moderate to severe cases of depression or anxiety. One or a combination of medications may be needed. These medications include: selective reuptake inhibitors such as fluoxetine, sertraline, paroxetine, and escitalopram, among others; atypical antidepressants such as venlafaxine, bupropion (also approved for the use of smoking cessation), and duloxetine (also approved for neuropathic pain); monoamine oxidase inhibitors (for treatment-resistant depression); and anxiolytics. The use of herbals such as St. John's Wort may be useful in mild to moderate cases of depression, and there is some evidence of the positive effects of Omega 3 Fatty Acids as adjunctive use in combination with FDA-approved antidepressants. Acupuncture and other naturopathic interventions may add value to the regimen. More research is required in these other areas.

Lifestyle Strategies

These interventions have become "complementary" in the Western world, when, in fact, they are an integral part of any medical intervention. You will find many lifestyle strategies while reading this book. Check the section on **The Four Pillars of Biological Health** (which include adequate nutrition, good sleep hygiene, regular exercise, and the practice of relaxation techniques on a regular basis) and the chapter on maximizing individual health and wealth strategies. My book *Managing Work in Life* gives you additional tips and strategies, and you will find even more ways of experiencing the power of well-being in the **Quantum Wellbeing** book and audiovisual series.

For more information about depression and anxiety disorders, please visit the following Websites:

- ☑ WORLD HEALTH ORGANIZATION: *www.who.int/en*
- ☑ NATIONAL INSTITUTE OF MENTAL HEALTH: *www.nimh.nih.gov*
- ☑ MENTAL HEALTH INFOSOURCE: *http://mhsource.com*
- ☑ AMERICAN PSYCHIATRIC ASSOCIATION: *www.healthyminds.org*

☑ NATIONAL DEPRESSION SCREENING DAY: *www.mentalhealthscreening.org*

☑ AMERICAN PSYCHOLOGICAL ASSOCIATION: *www.apa.org*

☑ MEDSCAPE: *www.medscape.com*

☑ WEBMD: *www.webmd.com*

Medical Interventions for Depression and Anxiety Disorders

☑ **Psychotherapy** (one or a combination):
   - ✓ Supportive.
   - ✓ CBT.
   - ✓ Intensive brief dynamic psychotherapy.
   - ✓ Psycho-education.

☑ **Psychopharmacology** (one or a combination):
   - ✓ Selective serotonin reuptake inhibitors (SSRIs).
   - ✓ Atypical antidepressants.
   - ✓ Monoamine oxidase inhibitors (MAOIs).
   - ✓ Anxiolytics.
   - ✓ Herbals (consult for combinations).
   - ✓ Complementary interventions (acupuncture and naturopathic interventions).

☑ **Lifestyle Strategies** (The Four Pillars of Biological Health):
   - ✓ Sleep.
   - ✓ Nutrition.
   - ✓ Exercise.
   - ✓ Relaxation.

LESSONS LEARNED FROM CHAPTER 2

1. **Stress is the buzzword of the 21st century.**

2. A **business coach** can help you maximize your performance and productivity by helping you set up and follow up on goals to achieve your desired outcome.

3. If you are already experiencing problems in your performance, productivity, or health, you need to **first fix the problem** before continuing to improve.

4. **Business** addresses improving performance and productivity from a normal baseline to improved performance and increased productivity.

5. **Healthcare** considers improving performance and productivity from a disease-to-health baseline.

6. **Lost productivity, absenteeism, and presenteeism cost** companies billions of dollars every year.

7. If you are already experiencing **medical-related problems related to stress**, such as uncontrolled high blood pressure, diabetes, headaches, depression, or panic attacks, you should **consider visiting your primary doctor** or a specialist before your medical condition worsens.

8. Consider a thorough **evaluation** by a professional when experiencing medical problems including anxiety or depression.

9. The best approach to **treat medical conditions** includes psychopharmacology, education, and lifestyle strategies.

10. The best approach to **treat depression or anxiety** disorders includes a holistic intervention including one or a combination of psychopharmacology for moderate to severe cases (medication management), psychotherapy, and lifestyle strategies.

Interview 2

"Efficiency"
DONNA SHALALA

This interview with the president of the University of Miami can be summarized with one word: *efficiency*. President Shalala is clear in her concepts. She is open, concise, and precise. She knows what she thinks and she delivers her concepts with self-assertion and without hesitation.

DONNA SHALALA ON LEADING UNDER PRESSURE

Shalala: It's hard for me to think of an example because I've always been leading under pressure. I've always been in that kind of a position.

Cora: *Was this by choice or by default?*

I think by default. I ended up in administration because it was a good job, and an opportunity to go to Washington. I went to Washington [D.C.] to be an assistant secretary at HUD [the Department of Housing and Development] in the 1970s and from there I went through three college presidencies before I went to Washington as a Cabinet post. Most of my adult life I have always been running things under pressure so it's hard for me to pick out a specific example that was pressure-filled because I've always had deadlines, I've always had people screaming at me, I've always had some economic crisis where we had to find some resources, cut the budget, or fire people...so there is no individual event.

Pressure has been a constant for you.

Yes, it's been a constant; I'm used to it. As a result, I'm probably the calmest person in the room.

Do you experience this calmness right when that difficult situation strikes, or do you deal with pressure in a fast way?

I've had a lot of experience, so, often I can deal with it very fast. But sometimes, it's so complex you need to let it sort itself out.

Probably the best advice I ever had was from a former mayor of New York, Robert Wagner. He said to me that many thought he was indecisive, but he believed that very complex issues sometimes had a timing. He felt you should sometimes put the rock on the ground and let it sort itself out by itself before you jumped on the issue and that was good advice.

How about when you needed to make a decision right away?

Often you have to make a decision based on what you know.

Most people manage multiple pressures; is there anything you would suggest to be more effective?

Yes: Be rested. I once told my staff that the president of the United States hired us for our judgment and not for our stamina, and that it was very important to be rested in these kinds of jobs because you were always under pressure.

I think that if you have high-pressure and high-profile jobs, people forget that working night and day doesn't mean you are going to make decisions better or quicker. Sometimes it's important to go home and sleep on it. You have to learn how to sleep on things and not let things keep you awake.

As a leader, you are in charge of your own stamina and you are in charge of others'.

That's exactly right. I'm always very conscious about making sure I don't bother people on weekends or that I keep them very late. I really think they can get their work done during the week.

You are very efficient and practical. Was this any different early in your career?

I was more anxious about everything. I certainly worked longer hours and less efficiently. I was more frightened when there was a crisis. Getting hit over the head and making the wrong decisions gave me the experience. Experience made a big difference and it's why I'm better now. Being used to making a decision helped, so experience is key.

Would you choose positions without pressure at this point?

No, I like messy positions; I just feed off of them; I strive under pressure.

Are there any specific skills you need to strive under pressure?

You have to be non-compulsive; you can't be a compulsive personality, otherwise you just tear yourself apart. You've got to assume you will win some and lose some.

Anything else that you would like to add in terms of your critical thinking process when confronting pressure?

The key is to make sure that everybody that has an opinion has given it to you so that you don't get stuck on an issue. Make sure that everybody knows that they should limit the ideas over the number of people in a room or you will run into trouble.

It's also important for them to see that you are calm.

Would you like to add anything else?

Shalala: That's it; this was fun!

Donna E. Shalala became President of the University of Miami in 2001. Born in Cleveland, Ohio, President Shalala received her BA degree in history from Western College for Women. One of the country's first Peace Corp Volunteers, she served in Iran from 1962 to 1964. She earned her PhD degree from The Maxwell School of Citizenship and Public Affairs at Syracuse University. She served in the Carter administration from 1977 to 1980 as Assistant Secretary for Public Development and Research at the U.S. Department of Housing and Urban Development. She served as president of Hunter College of the City University of New York from 1980 to 1987 and as chancellor of the University of Wisconsin-Madison from 1987 to 1993. In 1993 President Clinton appointed her U.S. Secretary of Health and Human Services (HHS) where she served for eight years, becoming the longest-serving HHS Secretary in U.S. history. At the end of her tenure as HHS secretary, *The Washington Post* described her as "one of the most successful government managers of modern times." In June 2008, President Bush presented her with the Presidential Medal of Freedom, the nation's highest civilian award.

CHAPTER 3

THE HEALTHY INDIVIDUAL

The World Health Organization defines health as a state of complete physical, mental, and social well-being, and not merely the absence of disease or infirmity. All effective interventions in medical psychiatry include the bio-psycho-social approach. As healthcare dollars have continued to shift toward expert and expensive procedures, preventive approaches to health and well-being have become segmented and limited. It is not uncommon for a busy executive or professional to have a physical evaluation by his or her internist, receive medication therapy from a psychiatrist, receive psychotherapy from a therapist, and receive coaching from someone else. This disintegrated approach forces the busy businessman or woman to remember what was said to whom, where, and when. Making everyone talk while in separate systems is one of the most significant challenges when providing care. The paradox lies in how to enhance a holistic approach while addressing specific needs at the same time.

If we consider our self as a system in full operation with structures (dimensions) and interactive processes (performance and productivity) working in full alignment and in unison, we will find the much desired system in balance. To optimize this process, we need to know the exact characteristics of the structure, its potential, and its deficiencies. If there is a problem in one area, the problem needs to be fixed in that same area. If one area or dimension is severely impaired or affected for an extended period of time, other dimensions will most likely be affected as well. The more severely impaired and the longer the impairment, the more structures and processes that may need to be repaired across dimensions.

An individual self has several systems or dimensions in operation, including the physical, intellectual, emotional, social, and spiritual. We can maximize our performance and productivity as active processes within each and every dimension. By better understanding each dimension we can improve and maximize our performance and productivity within each as we integrate our efforts in balancing our system.

In summary, the key dimensions include:

1. **Physical:** Our physical body.
    From an individual perspective, one of the most obvious and important areas that we must keep in prime shape is the physical dimension. Nutrition, sleep, exercise, and relaxation practices are the biological pillars of this area. The mission that we have designed for ourselves manifests on the physical plane.

2. **Emotional:** Our feelings and emotions.
    Next is the emotional dimension. This is the area where we experience feelings, and this area is further expressed by our ability to connect with others. Our relationship with family and friends makes our affective world rich and joyful.

3. **Cognitive:** Our mind and intellect.
    In this area there is training, education, and constant learning and skills training from a mental perspective. This is the area where our vision for the future is created.

4. **Social and Community:** Our interconnectedness with other people and with groups of people.
    As a person, our well-being and growth also depend on our ability to connect and interrelate with our community, our work organization, and other organizations and cultures.

5. **Spiritual:** Our values, ethics, love for art, and beliefs in a higher self and higher being.
    Lastly is the spiritual dimension, which includes our relationship with a higher being or connection with

our higher self through prayer, meditation, and self-awareness. This area includes volunteerism, altruism, and esthetics. This is the key area where our values reside. Our individual ethics connect to our value system within this area.

The active processes within each dimension include:

☑ Productivity

☑ Performance

Productivity and performance processes operate within each of these areas, allowing us to constantly improve within each dimension. The descriptions I've given apply to a personal or individual perspective, but we can use the same framework in regard to a healthy organization.

Figure 8: The Healthy Individual—Dimensions

Physical	Nutrition, sleep, exercise, relaxation, MISSION
Emotional	Relationship with family and friends
Cognitive	Constant learning, skills training, VISION
Social	Community, family organization, social support
Spiritual	Prayer, meditation, ethics, volunteerism, altruism, aesthetics, VALUES
Performance	Quality of work, self-assessment and feedback evaluation
Productivity	Work output, compensation

THE PHYSICAL DIMENSION

This is the dimension where our purpose and our mission are manifested into action. Although our mission doesn't generate in this dimension, it materializes here. This is the area where we are able to bring to life the expression of our ideas and abilities. We may have envisioned the most amazing worlds in our mind's eye (intellectual dimension), but unless we are able to transform these into action, they will just be a part of a "future project" rather than a tangible reality.

In addition to this very significant characteristic, the physical is the dimension responsible for offering us our greatest source of energy and stamina. This is one of the main reasons why it is so important to fix any health problem as soon as it arises, avoid artificial ways of increasing our energy, and continue to improve our health by improving our baseline state of physical health.

One of the first steps I offer my coaching clients and medical patients during our first session is to maximize their physical energy by setting up goals to improve the four biological pillars that contribute to our well-being:

1. Nutrition
2. Exercise
3. Sleep
4. Relaxation

When you can master each of these aspects of your physical health you will be able to endure the ups and downs of dealing with constant or periodic personal and organizational challenges. I am often asked about a "magical" recipe for leading under pressure. The biological strategy in the physical dimension is to maximize biology on a regular basis. This simple premise will help you bounce back to a good and healthy lifestyle during critical times.

The obvious, common-sense disclaimer comes next:

Consult your physician before making any significant lifestyle changes. I offer the following tips and strategies as general guidance.

I always custom-make programs for my clients and patients given their baseline state of health and fitness.

Nutrition

Obesity continues to be a public health concern in the United States and throughout the world, according to the Centers for Disease Control and Prevention. In the United States, the frequency of obesity doubled from 1980 to 2004. Obesity is associated with the increased risk of a number of conditions, including cardiovascular disease, hypertension, certain cancers, and diabetes. Although multiple factors may contribute to becoming obese, lack of exercise and overeating food with high caloric content are at the top of the list.

BMI, or body mass index, is the formula widely used to measure the full range from healthy weight through morbid obesity. BMI is equal to weight in kilograms divided by height in meters squared. Someone with a BMI of 25 to 29.9 is classified as overweight, 30 to 40 counts as obese, and people with BMIs of 40 or more are morbidly obese. For more information on overweight and obesity on the CDC Website, visit *www.cdc.gov/obesity/index.html*. The U.S. National Institutes of Health has an online BMI calculator at *www.nhlbisupport.com/bmi/*.

According to 2007 reports (data for 2005–2006) from the National Center for Health Statistics, one of the Centers for Disease Control and Prevention:

☑ 67% of non-institutionalized adults 20 years and over are overweight or obese.

☑ 34% of these adults are obese (about 72 million people).

☑ Approximately 65% of obese adults have been told that they are overweight.

The obesity epidemic may directly increase the risk of:

☑ Cardiovascular disorders such as hypertension and coronary heart disease.

☑ Endocrine disorders such as type 2 diabetes.

☑ Systemic disorders such as dyslipidemia, osteoarthritis, and certain cancers.

☑ Neurological Disorders such as Stroke and sleep apnea.

☑ Digestive Tract Disorders such as gallbladder disease.

We are what we eat, drink, and anything else we bring into our body.

Good nutrition is a key pillar, providing for our physical, mental, and emotional stamina. Food pyramids and nutrition guidelines have been insufficient in preventing our high rates of obesity in the United States. Whereas many "read" the caloric intake in "what" they eat, few people know "how" to eat well. Our culture craves the magic diet, inviting the trendiest diet guru to dictate the fashionable diet of the time. Instead of using common sense, many people drastically shift to an "all protein diet," then to an "all carbohydrate diet," and then to an "all vitamin diet," instead of looking for ways to balance a healthy diet. More are concerned about losing weight than about eating healthy.

In today's busy world, many people want to replace good eating habits with a bunch of vitamins, processed food, or the latest herbal potion. Unfortunately, I have seen too many depend on these concoctions, sometimes taking 25 or more pills a day, instead of focusing on scheduling a good food regimen. Some are taking these huge amounts of pills to "treat" underlying anxiety or depression and are reluctant to take an FDA-approved medication for their underlying medical problem. To make matters worse, some have entered the craze of avoiding natural carbohydrates because they have "heard" carbohydrates are bad for health. In the meantime, many are still not eating vegetables and fruits.

The bottom line is simple: Implementing a healthy diet demands discipline and adhesion to a schedule, period. Implementing a basic diet is a key ingredient for longstanding health and well-being. Balancing carbohydrates, fats, and protein is key and will depend upon each individual. As a rule of thumb, consider breakfast, lunch, and dinner as the essential structure of a healthy diet. Add three snacks in between if you will have hours without any food.

These are general suggestions for a healthy diet: they simply follow a rational and common-sense thought process. As a general rule, consider dividing the "awake" day in even intervals, say, four-hour intervals. That's right, I wrote "awake." You should not eat at night unless this is specifically recommended by your personal physician:

☑ 6–8 a.m.: Breakfast

☑ 11–2 p.m.: Lunch

☑ 5–8 p.m.: Dinner

The busy working person will benefit from having this schedule. At least two of your meals need to be comprehensive and well-balanced. Breakfast or lunch should be your strongest meals. Many executives are having just one meal a day these days, and this meal is often dinner. Meal times ought to be included in your schedule, just as you would include a business meeting or an appointment to hire a new employee. If you can eat at your facility, a 30-minute break will suffice. Consider meal times as sacred: it is very important that you sit down and focus on your meal rather than eat while you are checking your e-mail or catching up with work. A 10-minute break for a snack may suffice as well, using the same strategy. My preferred version of a healthy diet consists of a mildly modified proposition to Dr. Sears's Zone Diet: Eat up to four meals a day with two snacks, avoiding food craving. Consider your plates as a gourmet dish, not a double-size plate that would feed three people in countries other than the United States. Fill one third of your plate with a serving of lean protein about the size of the palm of your hand. Fill a third of your plate with vegetables (the more colorful mix, the healthier), and add olive oil. Fill the last third with small portions of rice, pasta, or legumes. Eat fruits or fruit salad before or after your meal or as snacks. A glass of natural juice will count as eating fruit. Use dried fruits and nuts as snacks throughout the course of the day (two or three times if you have three meals).

If you are struggling with carbohydrate craving including sweets, ice cream, or chocolate, consider having these only *after* you have had your meal. Avoid eating these alone, as you will have a higher chance of binging on them. There is no physiological need to eat while you sleep. If you are waking up in the middle of the night and visiting the refrigerator in hiding, consider this a good time to stop this habit. If you are having a hard time sleeping, you may consider taking tea or warm milk as you try to go back to bed. For additional resources about the food pyramid visit *www.mypyramid.gov*.

How about coffee? Can I drink coffee? And how much can I drink?

During the day, caffeinated drinks are best if taken in the morning, and should be avoided after 2 or 3 p.m. depending on your sleep time. If you decide to drink caffeinated drinks, consider avoiding drinking more than two drinks per day. Replace the drinks with non-caffeinated beverages. If you have been drinking too much coffee, you will need to wean yourself off, as caffeine is highly addictive. If you go down from four cups to one, for example, you may experience caffeine withdrawal. Withdrawal symptoms include headaches, irritability, vague pains, nervousness, fatigue, or sleepiness. My suggestion is the following:

Use a calendar. Assess your caffeine intake for a week to check exactly how much you are actually taking throughout the course of the day, and when. Your next step will be to cut your intake gradually: If you have been taking eight drinks per day, you may decrease in quantity by either reducing the serving amount or the times you drink per day. You may decrease the eight drinks by one cup every four to seven days, going down by one cup every four to seven days until you take one cup a day or none. Decide at what times you will continue to drink caffeinated drinks.

The other option is to cut down from a filled cup to 3/4 or 1/2 of a cup for four to seven days, then to 1/2 of a cup and so on, until you continue to take the two drinks at your desired times, no later than 3 p.m. It is not uncommon to see people struggling with generalized anxiety and/or panic attacks still drinking a considerable amount of caffeinated drinks. My suggestion is always to cut down and/or discontinue coffee altogether if the person is actively experiencing panic attacks.

I like to drink a glass of wine every night; is this a problem?

Although drinking a glass of wine during meals may be recommended, avoid drinking more than a glass of wine or its equivalent at night. Consider drinking in moderation in social gatherings and avoid drinking alone. The CAGE test acronym may help you identify whether or not drinking is a problem for you:

- ☑ Have you made attempts to CUT down on drinking?
- ☑ Are you ANNOYED by others' criticisms about your drinking?
- ☑ Do you feel GUILT about drinking?
- ☑ Do you use alcohol as an EYE-OPENER in the morning?

If you believe you are having problems with alcoholism, seek help.

If you find yourself in a cycle in which you are waking up in the morning and *must* drink coffee to wake up, and you believe you *must* drink alcohol to sleep at night, rest assured you have already entered the negative cycle in the life of the busy executive. You may be self-treating to gain stamina through coffee as your biological energy may be exhausted, and you may feel the need to drink alcohol to sleep, even if you feel exhausted yet unable to fall asleep at night.

The opening story in this book is a common reality in my practices: Too many of my clients or patients have had the experience of visiting the emergency room, scared of possibly having a heart attack when waking up with chest pain in the middle of the night. The pattern looks like this: The weeks before this event may have been preceded by increased amounts of pressure followed by more coffee or stimulants during the day and more alcohol to sleep at night. After a few hours of sleep, the person wakes up in the middle of the night, sweaty, agitated, and with feelings of pressure in their chest. Dead worried, they rush to the emergency room. After normal cardiograms and blood tests, the emergency room physician approaches the person and asks them if they have been experiencing much stress lately. The person may or may not recognize the stress. The ER doctor then suggests they visit a psychiatrist. This usually seems like the Twilight Zone to the person who just seems to be experiencing purely physical symptoms in the absence of psychological or cognitive ones. In the end, the panic attack may have very well been triggered by the triangle of stress, coffee, and alcohol.

Although coffee, alcohol, lack of sleep, overwork, exhaustion, and stress are not the underlying reasons for panic attacks, they can certainly play a significant role in creating an environment in which someone with the genetic predisposition will be likely to manifest anxiety or depression as their systems of resilience are exhausted.

How about power drinks?

Watch out, as pure sugar or pure caffeine may make you feel attentive yet wired and tense.

How about smoking?

Stop smoking, period. The good news is that most workplaces forbid smoking, and smoking is not allowed in most private places so quitting is made easier and easier, particularly in the United States. If you cannot stop on your own, consider nicotine gum, nicotine patches, FDA-approved medications (bupropion or varenicline), and/or hypnosis. If you have tried one of these before and it didn't work, consider trying a combination of them under your doctor's supervision. None of these will work unless you have decided to stop smoking. Only you can decide for yourself.

Exercise

Millions of Americans suffer from chronic illnesses that can be prevented or improved through regular physical activity. These conditions include:

- ☑ Cardiovascular disorders such as hypertension and coronary heart disease.
- ☑ Endocrine disorders such as type 2 diabetes.
- ☑ Obesity.

Exercise is another essential component of our formula to stay healthy. In the past, physical activity may have been more of an integral part of daily living; *now*, with increasing sedentary activities and inactive entertainment, the only way to counteract a passive lifestyle is through daily exercise.

In general, morning exercise is the most effective, relaxing, and energizing. Morning exercise allows us to start off fresh, increase our blood flow, increase our metabolism, and produce natural endorphins (neurotransmitters that make us feel good and decrease our pain perception). After exercising, our body may feel pleasantly relaxed physically, while mentally sharp, focused, and clear. Of course, if you believe the *only* time you can exercise is in the evening, do not hesitate to exercise then, particularly if that's the only time you can fit it into your busy schedule.

Relaxing exercises tend to be the most repetitive (and boring) ones: walking, cycling, rowing, running, jogging, spinning, cross-country skiing, and swimming. These are excellent exercises (and a must!) for busy executives who spend hours at sedentary work and for those who fly and travel as a part of their busy schedules. Yes, I know, not everyone finds these exercises boring. If you find them exciting, great for you!

It is even better if you can exercise outdoors. However, if the only way you can include cardiovascular exercises is at the gym or at your treadmill at home, don't hesitate to do this. The idea is to create a constant state of increased metabolism, as if you were running a marathon. By creating this elevated metabolic baseline you will feel more comfortable running the sprints you'll need to race throughout your busy executive or entrepreneurial venture. This is probably the closest analogy to the real life of the busy executive, in contrast to an "on and off" situation, such as a tennis match, a basketball game, or a football match.

If you find yourself reading light material such as gossip magazines (I've seen both men and women reading mindless magazines at the gym), I actually suggest quite the contrary. Your treadmill or elliptical time is a great time to read complex material. Why? Your blood flow is at its best, your focus at its peak, and you have undivided attention with no interruptions. Take advantage of this situation and read what you need to read, would like to read, or wouldn't be able to read at other times.

If you anticipate a more demanding work schedule, consider challenging yourself by increasing your strength. Weight-lifting or increased resistance exercises will enable you to increase strength. I have encountered people struggling with "how to exercise" more than with "what to do." The most common complaint is:

I have no time to exercise.

My response is simple, just as with your meal times. Let this be your mantra:

CREATE THE TIME

And make it happen.

No one else will make it happen for you.

If your workday just went from 12- to 16-hour days you won't have the luxury to cut down on exercise—quite the contrary. To sustain high levels of work and stress you should increase your exercise schedule instead of decreasing it. Unless your job demands regular physical activity, you must incorporate exercising in your daily living to remain fit and healthy. As an accomplished executive, you are constantly bringing work-related priorities to continue to succeed. Make sure exercising is one of them.

Start by exercising five minutes every day for the first week, particularly if you have not exercised in a long period of time or if you are overweight. Start slowly, and then increase the time to 10 minutes a day until you reach at least 30 minutes a day. Remember, there are two ways in which you can increase your physical output: with the intensity of the exercise (exercising faster or adding more strength), or extending the amount of time in which you exercise. Currently, 30 minutes of daily exercise is the minimum amount of exercise time recommended by the American Medical Association. You may want to consider some cardiovascular training most days, alternating with strength exercises. Flexibility exercises should be considered as an integral part of both cardiovascular and strength exercises. To learn more about cardiovascular, strength, or flexibility exercises, visit the American College of Sports Medicine at *www.acsm.org*.

Sleep

More than 40 million Americans suffer from sleep disorders. Excessive daytime sleepiness is responsible for thousands of deaths each year. Most people do not know that they suffer from a sleep disorder, which can be easily treated once recognized.

Sleep is the third component of the physical dimension. Many disregard the significance of maintaining good sleep hygiene. Many minimize the benefits of sleep and the essential properties sleep brings to our ability to produce and perform at our best. In addition, sleep dysregulation and stress can increase the risk for depression and anxiety. These problems may also have direct influence over the immune system and increase the risk for heart disease.

Stressed executives and business owners carry their worries and concerns to their sleep. As they can't relax and re-energize throughout the course of the night, they wake up tired and exhausted, unable to focus, further prolonging the negative cycle. In short: they are stressed out during the course of the day and stressed out during the course of the night.

In contrast, sleeping six to eight hours every night will enhance the person's physical, intellectual, and emotional energy. Having a "good night's sleep" will improve the individual's ability to concentrate during the course of the day, thus gaining control over activities and responsibilities.

It is imperative to exert discipline to sleep at regular intervals. You may need to find times to recover before your next trip if you travel frequently or, more so, if you travel across meridians. For example, instead of taking a red-eye to go to your destination and fly back that same day with another red-eye, make sure you can stay at a hotel, sleep overnight, and then catch the returning flight the following day. Additionally, consider avoiding giving a presentation, carrying a negotiation, or conducting business upon arrival after a long flight. Yes, I have met adventurers who have enjoyed pushing their stamina to the max. I have also seen executives doing this feeling obliged by corporate demands. I personally believe the executive will conduct business much better if well-rested, refreshed, clear-minded, and with an accurate sense of perception. The alternative is a hyper-alert, fatigued presenter or negotiator who will miss the full range of options because of physical and mental exhaustion.

In general, sleep cycles are best at night and wake cycles are best in daylight. Many are forced to sleep on alternate schedules. The more people are awake during daylight hours, the better they will be able to sleep. The more people are interrupted at night, the worse they will do during the day. Studies show a higher predisposition of heart problems only by virtue of interrupted sleep!

Avoid alcohol or prolonged use of hypnotics to induce sleep—prolonged use meaning more than two weeks. Watch out if you have already been in the negative loop of taking medications to sleep and stimulants to keep awake in the morning. If so, it is time to consider a thorough evaluation, as your system is demanding opposite interventions: an upper and a downer. Also, make sure you have not been increasing your alcohol intake to sleep at night (and then increasing your caffeine intake in the morning to counteract the effects of alcohol). I have seen too many panic attacks triggered by the alcohol withdrawal occurring in the middle of the night, about two to four hours after the last drink, to be precise.

These are some good practices conducive to good sleep:

☑ Try to set up a regular time to go to bed and a regular time to get up in the morning. If you travel, allow yourself to rest during your trip. Drink plenty of fluids, do some mild exercise in your seat every two or three hours, and try to accommodate to the new time schedule as soon as possible. Stay awake at your new destination until bedtime. If you are unable to fall asleep, try listening to soft music or a relaxation tape, or try breathing exercises. Avoid turning on the television, reading, or distracting yourself with anything that may further activate your brain activity, preventing you from going back to bed.

☑ Avoid taking daytime naps. Although some reports show a one-hour nap a day may be beneficial and refreshing, what is most refreshing is creating a transition from one intense activity to another. If you are extremely tired because of travel or any other challenges, avoid going to bed. Instead, consider taking a 15-minute nap in a sitting position, try a relaxation tape, or try breathing exercises. You may also practice Tai-Chi, Yoga, or Qi-Gong, or even dance to great music for 15 minutes if you have the energy to move. These strategies will help you bring your energy level up again.

☑ As mentioned before, avoid caffeine at least four to six hours prior to your bedtime. Avoid smoking or drinking to go to sleep. Avoid strenuous exercise close to your sleep time.

☑ Remember: the bedroom is for sleep and sex. You should not eat, read, or watch television in bed. Yes, I know, many people do. And many people also have problems with sleep, obesity, and their marriage.

For more information about sleep, visit The American Academy of Sleep Medicine Website at *www.aasmnet.org*.

Relaxation

Relaxation comprises the fourth element of the physical dimension. Sleep and exercise have a direct impact on enhancing a relaxed state. Additionally, listening to music, using guided imagery, painting, having a hobby, playing music, or singing may also contribute to achieving and living in a relaxed state, a state of balance. Practicing relaxation and meditation techniques on a regular basis can cause lasting beneficial effects in heart health, brain activity, and the immune system.

Too many people race through their days, leading aggressive lives to stay competitive, participating in exhausting meetings and activities, to then rush to a yoga class or a meditation session. During this time, they seem to allow themselves to become a different being, to then transform, once again, into the ever-assertive, go-getter, successful executive. How can this happen, and is this strategy effective at all? In a way, this approach is like pushing the body into roller-coaster mode, an on-off switch alternating from speed to Nirvana in a split second. Is this the answer?

It is vital to concentrate on each activity, one at a time, at the present moment, rather than driving in the car, listening to music, answering business calls on the cellular phone while writing on a pad, eating a sandwich, and punching in numbers to a PDA, all while driving! (I am not joking, some of my clients have shared with me they do this—or, I'd better say, they *used to* do this.) In essence, the trick is to be in the here and now, and nowhere else. Although it may seem as if executives are able to do all this successfully, it is inevitable the quality of each of these activities will not be the best. Although many people have the capability to do more than one thing at a time, it is not possible to give 100 percent to all activities at once. We can keep an eye on the total picture, but we can effectively manage only one activity at a time.

There are many available exercises and techniques of relaxation and disciplines helping a person achieve inner calm while living in a frantic schedule. I have consistently observed that people who can be "busy on the outside and calm on the inside" are capable of facing the toughest critical incidents and intervene in the most challenging situations. I refer to this state as **The Power of Wellbeing**. When my patients and clients reach this point, most describe feeling in peace, tranquility, bliss, alignment, balance, and a deep sense of well-being. Because they are living in this inner state, they feel connected with a profound source of energy. This energy—unlike the boost from artificial sources—is relaxed and holistic in nature.

You may want to maximize the use of relaxation techniques in the morning, throughout the course of the day as needed, and in the evening. Taking a few minutes throughout the day may help some. Others benefit more from taking a couple of periods throughout the day. Times for relaxation range from five minutes twice a day to 30 minutes one or more times throughout the day. Winding down toward the evening will enable you to sleep better at night as well.

Relaxation, guided imagery, and visualization techniques are powerful tools against physical signs of stress. Additionally, their positive effects may benefit the busy executive in a wide range of settings. These include the ability to create a state of calm at the start of the day and the opportunity to anticipate activities or events with the ability to resolve situations. Practicing relaxation techniques on a regular basis adds to the strategic toolbox of the traveling executive. As mentioned before, sleep and exercise enhances physical, intellectual, and emotional relaxation.

Listen to music or audio books daily while you drive; meditate or use guided imagery exercises daily when you wake up, during breaks, at night, or while you travel and are not driving. Learn techniques to visualize your day, your presentations, your learning, and your negotiations. The more you practice these techniques the better results you will have.

Although there are numerous relaxation techniques that you may want to practice, the most common induction techniques usually begin with deep breathing exercises, such as yoga breathing. Progressive relaxation and guided imagery techniques share a common general outline. If you travel often, take advantage of practicing these techniques, which you could apply while you fly, while you are about to travel, before going to sleep, or upon waking up. Consider doing these exercises regularly. The more you practice, the deeper state of relaxation you will achieve. The deeper the state, the easier it gets; the easier it gets, the deeper the state of well-being. Mastering this well-being experience will be experienced across dimensions: physical, emotional, intellectual, social, and spiritual.

You will find many relaxation tapes in the market. I have produced the **Quantum Wellbeing** series, available at *www. quantumwellbeing.com*. CDs and MP3 downloads are available to help you find your core (The Core), feel more relaxed while you travel (Flying Well), feel more relaxed prior to giving a presentation (Relaxed Presentations), and more.

THE EMOTIONAL DIMENSION

Our ability to experience emotions such as joy, frustration, confusion, boredom, passion, love, hate, fear, and distress will impact on our ability to relate with our loved ones, including our spouse, children, parents, siblings, extended family, friends, colleagues, bosses, and employees.

We relate with the world according to our own capacity to feel and experience on this deeper level. Stress, anger, or depression will impact negatively upon our experiences in contrast to joy, happiness, or living in a relaxed state. The importance of emotion in personal and social life is very complex. Specific parts of the brain are associated with different aspects of emotion.

"Emotional Intelligence," masterfully described by doctors Mayer and Salovey, and later published by Daniel Goleman in his book by the same name, is probably the most practical way of looking at emotion. Goleman argues that human competencies such as self-awareness, self-discipline, persistence, and empathy are of greater consequence than Intelligence Quotient (IQ) in much of life.

In a chaotic schedule and with managerial responsibilities, the successful executive and entrepreneur should master these human competencies and more, bringing these into practice at each and every level of their lives: at home, professionally, and within their organization. Expressing different emotions in different settings may be appropriate, and a sign of flexibility. On the other hand, if we are inconsistent, this action may take a toll on our relationship with others. If, by nature, we are empathic beings, and, at work, we feel the "need" to be cold and to hide our true selves, this lack of alignment will show in one way or another. People who can express their true emotions tend to achieve their greatest potential with ease. After all, they don't pretend to be someone they are not. The façade takes tons of energy and displacement that prevents us getting the job done. In addition, this lack of emotional alignment has brought many to public disgrace. Although the root of many of some politicians', artists', and athletes' infidelities lie in a split between the value they give their marriage and families, and the other life they are living. It is that emotional disconnect that has brought prominent figures under the gun. Managing the intensity or amplitude of emotions may be important for both individual and organizational reasons. Honoring your true emotion or feeling is key for alignment and long-lasting well-being.

I am still amazed at how many political leaders are chosen by gut feeling. "I don't like him or her," or its opposite, "I really like her or him" will come to play a significant role in elections, resulting in choosing someone who is well-liked instead of someone who is well-qualified! This is one of the same reasons why someone who is adored and placed on a pedestal—because of no reason but this emotional factor—will later be despised if fallen from grace, as in very public cases of infidelity or fraud.

A constantly stressful environment may impact upon our emotional expression. Interestingly, although someone may look calm and polite with his or her peers or superiors, he or she may treat others of lesser power with disrespect. For that reason, some company executives and smart business owners evaluate others' ability to relate to waiters, drivers, assistants, and employees. One person may be a refined aristocrat in a social setting, and switch to a Cruella at the steering wheel. If you believe you are in good shape and find yourself snapping at others with less power than yourself, watch out, as your emotional stability may only be a façade. You may want to seriously look into improving your relationship with others, exerting your own control, and truly treating others with respect. It will only come back to you as respect and trust.

Make an effort to treat your family members, friends, colleagues, and everyone within your organization with respect. Even-temper your relationship with everyone within your organization. Remember: You are able to do your job well because of all the support you receive from each and every member of your organization, from your cleaning staff to your most sophisticated strategy team guy or gal. This is another reason why implementing healthy lifestyle strategies will help you further improve this area—most people would turn into a despot if wired on coffee and sleep deprivation.

If you feel you are well-aware of your emotions and that you express them at the right place and at the right time, you are on your positive path. If, instead, your natural tendency is to feel negative about everything (spouse, children, family, work, and/or life), you may benefit from seeking psychotherapy to shift into a more positive outlook on life. Imagine this: If you are constantly feeling negative emotions and you are already expecting bad things to come your way, you are 100 percent correct! Life *will* bring you back the negative you are expecting, as your perception is ready for the bad things to come. This happens over and over again in spousal, parental, employee, and employer relationships. Cognitive-behavioral techniques will help you identify negative automatic thoughts and pre-established thinking patterns and shift them to more positive expressions and behavior. Although these techniques are initiated in the cognitive or intellectual dimension, they will impact upon your emotional world. You can convince yourself your spouse—or employee—is the worst or the greatest asset in your life. Focus on the positive attributes and allow yourself to feel the experience in its depth and magnificence.

THE COGNITIVE DIMENSION

Our intellectual ability has a strong genetic component and is shaped and expanded by our capacity to learn. Our IQ will define our base mental capabilities. The brain retains its plasticity or its ability to rewire itself for better function throughout life. Brain exercises play an important role in this rewiring process.

Many in corporate America are willing to hire people according to their degrees and past job history, but others will hire the smartest, to bring about innovative and creative ideas to the workplace. Open to the ability to learn and continue to improve.

For example, have you noticed how long it would take you to read an article addressing a new concept in an area that you are not familiar with in contrast with an article in an area in which you are an expert? You may efficiently scan the familiar article and take a snapshot of the core message, whereas you may need to read the unfamiliar article a couple of times to understand the concept.

Challenging ourselves to continue to improve in this dimension includes studying novel areas. For example, if we are experts in communications, we may benefit by pushing ourselves to study areas in math or finance. Studying a new language or learning about different cultures may be beneficial exercises as we challenge ourselves to the next level.

Although there is a significant generation gap in the use of technology, most people will benefit from learning new computer skills or from expanding information technology aspects of their work. If we constantly use the same computer programs we may still want to challenge ourselves by learning these programs more in depth or by learning additional programs. It is obvious we will benefit from delegating activities that need to be done to maximize our efficiency at work, and we should concentrate on doing what only we do best and what nobody else can do for us. As we learn new skills our mental activity enhances excitement and curiosity. Furthermore, by learning more we facilitate additional associations and connections within our brains, further expanding our ability to grow.

111

If you believe you have major gaps in specific areas, attempt to improve your knowledge by studying on your own, taking online courses, taking classes, or taking courses that will improve your knowledge. Identify your best way to learn: do you learn best by listening, seeing, interacting, or doing? The more you can combine these ways, the better. If you are hyper-focused solely on your work, create the time to learn new things in areas outside of your comfort zone. Challenge yourself.

Challenge Your Memory

What is all the hype about *brain fitness*? This term is used as it relates to creating a mental exercise plan to keep our memory sharp and stimulated. Studies have shown that those people who exercise their brains regularly will enhance problem-solving abilities, have the ability to think faster, and improve their reasoning and logical skills. Conversely, if the brain is not regularly challenged, it can grow weak and its functions will eventually decline. Most importantly, by regularly exercising your brain, you could be protecting yourself from the development of brain-related illnesses including dementia.

As you age, challenging your memory through the introduction of new experiences will help you awaken the unused areas of the brain, enabling it to function better. Consider trying simple activities such as tasting new foods, learning a new language, learning to play an instrument, or driving a different route to work. There are therapies and exercises that you can do to preserve and even improve your memory. You must challenge your mind on a regular basis to gain brain power. It is unnecessary to spend hundreds or thousands of dollars in software programs that "sell" a way to improve your memory. Instead, a common suggestion to my clients and patients is to focus on the five senses and to introduce something new on a regular basis. For example, you may want to try a new ethnic dish the next time you go out to eat (taste), choose a new type of music to listen to instead of your traditional choice (sound), go to another section at the art museum instead of the one you always visit (sight), recognize

112

new herbs and spices (smell), or try new experiences. For more exercises, visit *www.challengeyourmemory.com*.

How About Vision?

The intellectual dimension is also the area where vision originates. As an example, an idea may come to mind as a vision in a split second. If we believe this great idea will benefit many people, our vision is enhanced by our ability to place this vision into a rational, logical, and linear statement (intellectual dimension). When in alignment, this vision will inspire people to act for the greater good (spiritual dimension). The charismatic leader will share his or her passion (emotional connection) with his or her team. The leader then connects with the company or public at large (social dimension), and finally aligns the vision with the mission into action (physical dimension).

THE SOCIAL DIMENSION

This is the dimension of individual interconnectedness with groups beyond our comfort zone of family and friends. Our ability to understand our role in our community, in our environment, in our country, and in our world plays a significant part as we connect with larger groups. This relationship is enhanced at each and every level: school, college, clubs, and teams as we are growing up, adding work and organizations as we become adults. Our ability to establish one-on-one relationships with groups versus establishing networks of interactions will enhance our well-being as well as the well-being of those organizations—and people—with which we connect. This dimension is particularly important as a source of work opportunities or support when facing critical situations. Many relate to others through church groups, clubs, or other professional groups that share something in common, most likely a common mission. Our contributions on a social level take our needs and wants beyond our own individual needs and wants. Healthy individuals establish meaningful relationships beyond their comfort zone.

If you want to enhance your social health, consider identifying local groups that you may be interested in joining individually or as a family. Consider joining a professional association or business group and become an active participant. Avoid joining too many groups, as this will only disperse your focus and add unnecessary stress. Take the opportunity to network with associations and groups. Take networking opportunities that align with your overall plan, but avoid being in one networking activity after the other without getting things done.

THE SPIRITUAL DIMENSION

Many have overlooked this dimension in the past for fear of not being considered seriously. Many are still scorned by others if perceived to be overly religious. Whereas many governments and corporations have ridiculed people for their beliefs, others have disregarded the significance of this dimension, which hosts our value system. Although several religions have dictated value systems, some of them have also cultivated a culture of dependency through fear and hatred. But religion aside, our values include our ethics, principles, and morals. Altruism, aesthetics, and our ability to connect with our higher self or a superior being resides in this dimension. Whether we are religious, spiritual, Mystic, Agnostic, or Atheist, our belief system—closely intertwined with the intellectual dimension—interrelates with the spiritual dimension. When our individual values are not aligned with our organizational values there is distress at the core, manifested and experienced in the emotional dimension.

Identify your essential values. You may improve your own connection within the spiritual dimension through prayer, meditation, volunteerism, altruistic activities, or by enjoying the arts. Bringing a touch of aesthetics to everything you do will add to the spice. We are only able to experience **The Power of Wellbeing** when we live our lives in full alignment.

Figure 9: The Healthy Individual—Integration

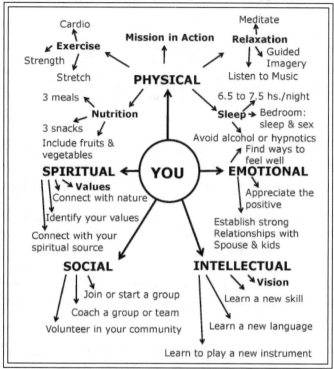

Interview 3

"Commitment"
GARY HOOVER

I met Gary Hoover at a global event of Entrepreneurs' Organization in Marrakech a few years ago. His keynote was fascinating. Aside from his obvious genius manifested through his amazing intellect and creative spirit, Gary is generous with his time and is constantly mentoring others. He maintains a list of new business ideas, containing more than 100 concepts as reported in *Fortune Small Business Magazine*. He subscribed to *Fortune Magazine* at the age of 12, convinced that the best way to make a positive change in the world was by leading or creating enterprises. By 18, he had already visited hundreds of corporate headquarters and offices. His question was the same: "What separates the losers from the winners?"

GARY HOOVER ON LEADING
UNDER PRESSURE

Hoover: You always learn. You'd better, or else it's a total loss. There's no question that an awful lot of successful businesses and even successful artists come from constraints like past failures: the fact that you have limited resources, or the fact that you didn't make that big sale, or the fact that the venture capitalists wouldn't bank you. The man who created QuickBooks had to do it himself because no one would fund him. That's the reason he did it the way he did it and he was so successful. Sam Walton couldn't sell his idea of small discount stores so he was cornered into doing it on his own. The founder of Home Depot had just been fired, and, in an act of desperation, created Home Depot. Yes, being constrained or having what are, at the time, constraints, can lead to innovation and creation.

116

Cora: *Is there any one instance when you were facing a very challenging situation like this?*

I have so many of them. One of the early ones was, I had a dream of creating this great big book superstore. Big store, big selection at low prices, which hadn't been invented yet. Mine was the first one. And I wanted to build a great big huge one in Chicago called Book City, and I needed somewhere in the three-million-dollar ballpark (or north of that) for it. I'd learned how to be in retail, I'd researched the industry for about seven years, and I was all ready to go. I showed it to some venture capitalists and they said, "You're crazy. The average book store does $80,000 a year and you want to do a million even; you're crazy." So, they all thought I was crazy.

One venture capitalist said, "Well, you know, if you copy this other person's concept (there was another small discount store starting out at the time but they didn't have many titles and didn't have a good selection, since my model was more like Toys "R" Us). He said, "If you give me an idea like that, I'll finance it." But I said, "No, that's really not what I'm talking about. You don't get it." So I said no, and borrowed money from my girlfriend for travel expenses. I had no money; I'd quit my job. I said, "What do I have to do to prove these guys wrong? They all think I'm nuts but I think I'm right."

So I had to reengineer the whole concept and I figured I had to do it in a smaller city or I could advertise everything for less capital, maybe with a bit of a smaller store (but still big selection at low prices).

Demand for books is related to education levels; education levels are highest in college towns. It couldn't be a really small college town, like College Station, Texas, or Columbia, Missouri, because they weren't big enough to support any bookstores. So it had to be a big college town. I figured either Ann Arbor, Michigan; Madison, Wisconsin; or Austin, Texas. I picked Austin because it was the fastest-growing and had the weakest competition. The guy who wanted to work with me to create the company also lived in Dallas. We came here and started a bookstore called BOOKSTOP. But instead of raising $3 million, we raised $350,000. We opened up and did a million eight the first year, and we were on our way. Not that we didn't have huge hurdles and sleepless nights down the pike, but, seven years later, we were the fourth biggest bookstore chain in the country. We sold to Barnes and Noble, which was their big entry into the bookstore business.

How did you react when people told you that they didn't understand your concept and that you wouldn't succeed?

I spent seven years developing the concept, so I knew a heck of a lot more about it than they ever did! I remember coming out of one venture capitalist's office—he had met with me in California—and he said, "Look, I'm really interested. Meet me in New York next month." That trip was all on borrowed money. So I'm in New York to see him and he says, "Oh, no, I'm not going to do it. I'm not interested in your concept."

I went to a Bun-and-Burger type place in New York City. I sat at that joint, ordered either a Coke or a glass of beer (I don't remember which), and I just moped. I had a couple drinks for about three hours, until I had to go catch my plane home.

I remember that very night I had a party. I was going back to St. Louis to see my old employer and my coworkers, and my girlfriend. I didn't know what to say to them because I knew they were all saying, "He's going to get the money." So here I was, coming back without the money and I was going to be all down in the dumps at the party. Sure, I thought about not going to the party, but I knew I couldn't do that. I said, "They'll know what happened anyway so you might as well face up to your disasters." In a recent article I did in which I spoke about failure, the really important thing is that it's natural to go home and mope. But the real question is: Do you mope for 30 minutes or 30 days... or 30 years!

I *knew* that giant bookstores were just going to happen, whether I did it or somebody else did. So to me, the only thing

I could do was run from the big company and go do my own thing.

When you commit yourself to something, you're married to it. I would talk to strangers on planes all the time about my ideas. I'd ask them, "What do you think of this idea," to get their reaction. But there is a point early on at which—when I have a new idea, when it's at a very early stage and I'm trying to decide whether to do this or not—that's the time I look a stranger on a plane in the eye and I say, "I'm going to go start this." That's a conscious step on my part.

One thing about being an entrepreneur is that if you have a regular job, you can quit. I could walk out right now from any of the three big companies I work for. I could do it without feeling that bad about it, right?

Here, that's *not* an option. You're the founding CEO. You can't turn to your company and say, "Oh, your time is up." That's just not an option. That process of, "Are you committed or not?" is important, but you've got to make that decision inside your head pretty early on. My time is way too valuable for me to go down a blind alley for a long period of time.

Gary Hoover travels the world speaking to Fortune 500 executives, trade associations, entrepreneurs, and college and high school students about how enterprises are built and how they stand the test of time. At the age of 30, he created the pioneering book superstore BOOKSTOP, which helped change the nature of book shopping in America. This company was sold to Barnes & Noble for $41.5 million cash when it was seven years old, and became a cornerstone for their industry-dominating superstore chain, which in 2007 did more than $4.5 billion in sales out of 700-plus stores. After selling BOOKSTOP, he began a small business information publisher, the Reference Press, a company that evolved into Hoover's, Inc., the world's largest Internet-based provider of information about enterprises. In 1999, Hoover's went public. It was purchased by Dun & Bradstreet for $117 million in 2003.

CHAPTER 4

HEALTH & WEALTH QUADRANTS FOR THE INDIVIDUAL

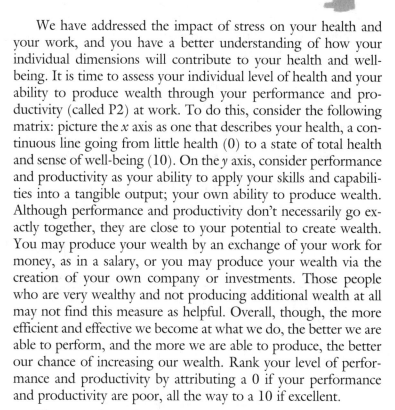

We have addressed the impact of stress on your health and your work, and you have a better understanding of how your individual dimensions will contribute to your health and well-being. It is time to assess your individual level of health and your ability to produce wealth through your performance and productivity (called P2) at work. To do this, consider the following matrix: picture the *x* axis as one that describes your health, a continuous line going from little health (0) to a state of total health and sense of well-being (10). On the *y* axis, consider performance and productivity as your ability to apply your skills and capabilities into a tangible output; your own ability to produce wealth. Although performance and productivity don't necessarily go exactly together, they are close to your potential to create wealth. You may produce your wealth by an exchange of your work for money, as in a salary, or you may produce your wealth via the creation of your own company or investments. Those people who are very wealthy and not producing additional wealth at all may not find this measure as helpful. Overall, though, the more efficient and effective we become at what we do, the better we are able to perform, and the more we are able to produce, the better our chance of increasing our wealth. Rank your level of performance and productivity by attributing a 0 if your performance and productivity are poor, all the way to a 10 if excellent.

These are the options:

- ☑ **Quadrant I:** Low Health and Low Performance and Productivity (P2)
- ☑ **Quadrant II:** Low Health and High P2
- ☑ **Quadrant III:** High Health and High P2
- ☑ **Quadrant IV:** High Health and Low P2

This exercise will allow you to first assess your current individual situation in the health and wealth matrix. The more accurate the assessment, the easier it will be to create your plan of action and implement successful strategies to improve your health or your performance and productivity. Next, we will discuss effective strategies you can apply depending on the quadrant where you are. Some of these strategies are specific to helping you improve your health, and some are specific to helping you improve your performance and productivity. Choose the strategies that best apply to you and implement them in your daily activities both at home and at work.

This is one of the many strategies I use when assisting executives and entrepreneurs. I use many more ways of assessing levels of health, performance, and productivity in **Managing Work in Life**. More information is available at *www.managingworkinlife.com*.

Figure 10: Individual Quadrants

	LOW HEALTH HIGH P2	HIGH HEALTH HIGH P2
PERFORMANCE & PRODUCTIVITY	**II**	**III**
	I	**IV**
	LOW HEALTH LOW P2	HIGH HEALTH LOW P2

THE HEALTH CONTINUUM

INDIVIDUAL QUADRANT I (IQI): LOW HEALTH, LOW P2

Mary is in her late 50s. She is widowed and has struggled with problems with her health for some years, and, more recently, with her finances. She has arthritis, moderate levels of recurring depression, and vague aches and pains described by her physician as fibromyalgia. When Mary's husband was alive, she was a housewife, bringing up her three now-grown children, who are currently all professionals. Although she has some savings and money available from her late husband's retirement, Mary faced the need to take a job to pay the bills, as she takes pride in being financially independent. Although she had studied years ago and was good at managerial jobs, she last worked decades ago, and is not familiar with the latest in computers. Although her work ethics are impeccable—she comes to work on time and she tries to do well—Mary has trouble keeping up with the amount of work, and the quality of her work, although good in effort, fails to reach her boss's expectations, as there always seems to be something missing...

Assessment

People in this category may be acutely or chronically ill, affecting their performance and productive capacity, and, potentially, impacting upon wealth. Even if the person is wealthy, many resources will need to be allocated toward health-related needs, further impacting upon future wealth. This sector includes untreated medical conditions, people on disability, or people who have been recently struck by a major illness or accident. One clear example in this area involves obesity-related medical problems, including diabetes and hypertension. Any attempt to lower blood pressure and glucose levels without implementing strategies to improve nutrition and exercise will be futile. Many people in

123

this quadrant are in the process of becoming disabled or are on disability. This quadrant includes increased levels of absenteeism (being absent from work) and presenteeism (being present at work but unable to perform because they are not feeling well).

Strategies

Prioritize your health, as you won't be able to focus on improving your performance until you feel better. It may feel overwhelming to attempt to fix what may seem to be many problems. Restore your health to a comfortable level before learning new skills. Next, coach and implement development skills in specific job areas after the health-related issues have improved.

1. Consult a physician. Make sure you have the right diagnosis for your medical condition. Ask your doctor and assisting healthcare practitioners about treatment options including medication and alternative therapies.

2. Many people in this category have both physical and psychological problems related to chronic conditions. Ask your doctor for a referral to a trusted psychiatrist. If your doctor has already initiated treatment with an anti-depressant to help you deal with co-morbid depression, consider having a consult with a psychiatrist and starting cognitive-behavioral therapy to support your treatment. Establish goals along the way and work on meeting your deadlines to continue to improve.

3. Start treatment. Consider holistic interventions: medication management, if necessary; rehabilitation; physical therapy; and alternative interventions. If you are dealing with pain, obesity, diabetes, high blood pressure, or other chronic medical conditions, you will benefit from maximizing **The Four Pillars of Health**.

4. If you are not exercising, start some kind of exercise; increase your physical activity by walking every day and build it from there. If you have not exercised in a long time, start walking five or ten minutes a day and increase by five or ten minutes every week as you add from there.

124

5. Eat healthy. Add vegetables and fruit to your diet. Avoid fried food and food with high caloric content. Add fish and olive oil to your diet. If you need a special diet, develop the discipline to follow it. Eat at regular intervals and times. If you want to lose weight, start by serving smaller portions on your plate.

6. After you are able to take better care of your physical health, focus on improving your work. If you are not at your physical, emotional, or mental best, your state will show in the quality or quantity of work you are able to produce.

7. Talk to your boss or your partners and work on improving one aspect of your work at a time. If you feel there are many areas you need to improve, prioritize your needs and focus on one, without moving to the next until you have improved.

8. Work with others so as to improve your cross-collaboration. Oftentimes two or three people may be working on activities that overlap, and would benefit from working together.

9. Understand your physical limitations but continue to focus on improving little by little. Even if you feel as though your road to recovery is long and tedious, you can always concentrate on breaking the work down into smaller parts that you can achieve one step at a time.

10. Once you have noticed improvement in one area, start improving the next one. Seek feedback and continue to improve. Avoid improving too many things at the same time. Once you are able to experience the positive effect of succeeding even one step at a time, it will become easier and easier.

Figure 11: IQI—Low Health, Low P2

> **ASSESSMENT:**
> Acutely or chronically ill.
> Untreated medical conditions.
> Low performance and productivity.
> Low wealth.
> **STRATEGIES:**
> Improve health first.
> Coach and development skills training next.

INDIVIDUAL QUADRANT II (IQII): LOW HEALTH, HIGH P2

Mark is in his 50s. As CEO of his own company, he has always worked like three people instead of one. He has always bragged about this ability of his. He was always able to manage many challenges simultaneously. In the past few years, though, he has noticed an increase in his responsibilities, and, although full of energy, he's also noticed he tires more than he used to. He has increased his coffee intake throughout the day to pump up his energy to be able to produce at the very high level he's used to producing. He has gradually increased his daily hours to 16 working hours and will sometimes extend his waking hours to meet incredible deadlines. Although he was an athlete in his high school and college years, his lifestyle has become more sedentary, with the occasional brisk, sports-related activity with business colleagues. Although drinking socially has always been a part of his business activities, lately, he has also felt the need to increase his glass of wine to two or three, accompanied by hard drinks at night to "relax" and sleep better. Some failed business and family stressors have added to his daily responsibilities. He has recently experienced more tension when dealing with ongoing personal and business relationships. Some people see him as being moody, while his family describes him as cranky. His wife and children have gradually become more distant from him, somewhat becoming indifferent to his constant complaining of his stress at work. He has noticed this distance and he attributes his pressure to needing to work more to keep the family's lifestyle. Mark has recently experienced a couple of events of waking up sweaty at night, heart pumping fast, perspiring profusely. He refused to go to the emergency room, as he is a strong believer he can deal with anything on his own...

Assessment

This is the most common area for high-functioning executives and entrepreneurs to burn out. They are still performing and producing on a very high level but only with the assistance of artificial performance enhancers. In this area, the individual is acutely or chronically ill (mild to severe). This area includes untreated medical conditions or ongoing uncompensated stress. In spite of being ill, the individual is still performing and producing at a high level. In the past, this individual may have worked like two, three, or four individuals, and only she or he may have noticed the decrease in performance or productivity. This is where many may have experienced burnout and energy depletion, subsequently facing more problems including panic attacks, depression, or other stress-related medical conditions. This group has fallen into the negative cycle of using stimulants during the day (culturally accepted, prescribed, or illegal drugs), and hypnotics at night to maintain performance and productivity at the highest possible level.

Strategies

If you find yourself within this quadrant, prioritize your health improvement process, put yourself first on your list beyond the "to do" list. If the health component continues to deteriorate, your health status may rapidly plummet into Quadrant I. Maximize your **Four Pillars of Biological Health**. Manage stress. Avoid caffeine and alcohol in excess, and, if you smoke, stop smoking.

1. Consult your physician and get a comprehensive physical examination as a baseline. Check your heart and brain health. Include blood tests, an electrocardiogram, a gynecology exam for women, and every additional age- and/or risk-recommended tests. Consider adding a nutritional and fitness evaluation to establish your baseline.

2. Reprioritize your work and integrate healthy habits in your hectic work world. Add exercise, meals, sleep, and relaxation time to your daily, weekly, and monthly calendars. Treat these times as if you were conducting business.

3. Cut down on caffeinated drinks and excessive drinking. Drink up to two caffeinated drinks per day, and no later than 2 p.m. You may drink up to two drinks (wine or beer) during the day, but avoid drinking altogether if you are already experiencing medical-related problems aggravated by using an upper (coffee) and a downer (alcohol). If you struggle with alcoholism, consult your physician and consider joining Alcoholic Anonymous meetings.

4. Avoid taking stimulants. Many successful executives and entrepreneurs start taking culturally accepted stimulants (coffee), then increase to over-the-counter medications and power drinks, then to prescribed amphetamines to increase their ability to perform. Avoid using drugs such as cocaine. If you struggle with drugs, consult your physician and consider joining Narcotics Anonymous meetings.

5. Start exercising 30 to 60 minutes a day with repetitive exercises (walking, jogging, cross-country skiing, rowing, or biking). If possible, exercise first thing in the morning. Exercise will help your body relax and will help

you focus your mind. Exercise in the evening if you can't exercise in the morning.

6. Eat three meals a day and three snacks every day. Make breakfast or lunch the strongest meal of your day. Keep your meals light but nutritious. Carry snacks so as to avoid being hungry between meals.

7. Start to practice relaxation techniques regularly: meditation, guided imagery, or listening to music. Use these as transitions between work and home, home and work, or in between intense activities. Consider 20-minute periods of transitions or Power Breaks.

8. Sleep at least six hours every night. It's best if you can sleep six to eight hours every night. Avoid watching television, particularly the news, right before you go to bed. Avoid doing or reading anything that would activate instead of relax your brain. This is another transition from a busy day at work to a quiet sleep ritual.

9. Spend time with your family. Many executives and entrepreneurs in this quadrant feel disconnected from their spouses and children because they *are* disconnected from their spouses and children. The earlier you can establish significant connections with your family the easier it will be to reestablish these deep relationships that have much fueled the reason why you work so hard. Have dinner as a family. Though some prefer to avoid eye-to-eye contact while carrying on a conversation in the car, nothing beats face-to-face interaction with your loved ones.

10. Take some time off on weekends and every few weeks. You may not have taken any time off for months or years. If you haven't done this at all, you may want to start by taking a day off before a holiday and having a four-day mini vacation.

Figure 12: IQII—Low Health, High P2

ASSESSMENT:

Acutely or chronically ill.

Untreated medical conditions.

High performance and productivity.

High wealth.

STRATEGIES:

Improve health—evaluate and treat underlying condition.

Manage stress.

Avoid caffeine and alcohol in excess.

Improve the Four Pillars of Health.

INDIVIDUAL QUADRANT III (IQIII): HIGH HEALTH, HIGH P2

Max is a professional businesswoman in her 40s. She has effectively juggled personal and professional responsibilities, both leading a successful business and experiencing positive interactions with her family. She had the experience of being close to burnout several years earlier. At the time, she made a major lifestyle change. She felt she had little choice but to do this as she came to terms with her family history of unhealthy lifestyle choices and shorter life spans. Since then, Max has experienced times in which she was able to produce at a high level even while experiencing extreme stress at the job. At other times, she struggled, particularly when facing a new business project. She is now able to self-regulate her personal and professional needs and wants, and she feels quite comfortable as she prioritizes responsibilities, needs, and wants on a personal and professional level. She has learned to nicely say no along the way, and, although many people see her very involved in multiple activities, she strongly believes she has an ultimate plan that puts it all together. Max has mastered the key to constant improvement; she incorporates changes and new challenges one at a time: Once she has been able to Improve, Achieve, and Maintain her desired goal, she moves on to her next level. She experiences joy in her personal life and in her work, as she believes she does what she was meant to do. 🎏

Assessment

Max is the ultimate corporate athlete. In this quadrant, the individual is healthy or has medical issues under control. The individual maintains a high level of performance and productivity. In this example, Max juggles multiple responsibilities but is able to prioritize her diverse activities and integrate them in an aligned plan. Although Max still faces constant pressure at work or at home as a part of her position at her job and in life, she has the ability to experience well-being while being very busy at the same time.

Strategies

Identify the healthy strategies that work for you and continue to use them to continue to improve your health and wealth situation. Establish specific goals to continue to improve within each and every area. Maximize **The Four Pillars of Biological Health** and challenge yourself along the way. If implementing new strategies, do this by bringing in one at a time. Improve, Achieve, and Maintain are core elements of **AIM I AM**. This concept is further described in the following chapter and in **Managing Work in Life**.

1. Maximize **The Four Pillars of Biological Health**: Exercise one hour a day. At this stage of working efficiently and effectively, as you take on more responsibilities, you will need to produce more energy in a natural way. Try a cardiovascular exercise for 30 to 60 minutes and add weight training to increase your strength.

2. If you are about to undertake a new business or job opportunity—and this is the best quadrant from which to do this—add some weight training to your schedule. If you feel as though you need to be in a highly competitive environment and your business is getting tougher, consider practicing martial arts. Its benefits include discipline, focus, physical exercise, and strategy. Avoid high-contact sports and unnecessary sports-related injuries.

3. Eat three meals and three snacks a day. Eat at the same time every day and start with breakfast or lunch as your main meal. The other meals may be lighter. Carry snacks to avoid long hours without meals. (A palmfull of mixed nuts and dried berries is my favorite.)

4. Ensure that you sleep six to eight hours every night. If you are very busy and need fewer hours of sleep at times, make sure you go back to your regular sleep schedule as soon as possible.

5. Practice relaxation techniques and continue to create effective transitions from home to work and from work to home or between intense and diverse activities. Listen to your favorite music every day. Better, listen to high-energy music for 10 to 20 minutes before starting a demanding project. Use music, meditation, or guided imagery exercises between demanding work. Call these your Power Breaks.

6. Check your current business plan and fine tune for further growth. If you don't have an emergency or succession plan, take the time to create one now, when things are going well. Many executives or business owners don't pay as much attention as they should. When you are fully operating in IQ3 you can easily determine what works and what may not be working as well within your organization. This is the best time to evaluate your plan and improve it so as to go on to the next level.

7. Learn and develop a new skill that will either help you feel well and/or that will help you in your job or business

(a new language, finances, learning technique, or musical instrument). This may be the best time to start the hobby you have been waiting to start for years. You need to continue to prioritize and manage your time, but if you feel you are in good control of your activities, see how you can integrate one additional skill or action that will benefit you either on a personal or business level.

8. Expand your personal and business connections via joining a new business, networking group, or professional organization. Connect beyond your comfort zone to expand your horizons. Hire a coach to move on to your next level of performance and productivity, or join a mastermind group with like-minded individuals who share your values, activities, or goals.

9. Continue to cultivate your relationship with family and friends. If you are on IQ3 you are experiencing healthy interactions with your family, extended family, and friends. Add one activity that will further help you connect with your spouse, your children, your parents, your siblings, and your friends.

10. Contact your extended family or good friends you haven't called for a while. Make it your purpose to call at least three people you care about weekly.

Figure 13: IQIII—High Health, High P2

ASSESSMENT:

Healthy or doing well under medical control.

High performance and productivity.

STRATEGIES:

Identify and continue to use successful strategies for health & wealth.

Establish goals to continue to improve in each and every area (exercise, nutrition, sleep, relaxation).

133

INDIVIDUAL QUADRANT IV (IQIV): HIGH HEALTH, LOW P2

"
Steve was a stellar worker on the technical end: well-respected, dependable, and a great colleague to others within his group. Management liked him for his reliability and his agreeable disposition, as he used to comply with whatever he was asked to do and he would always complete his job. When a more senior colleague stepped down as a manager, Steve was appointed by upper management to fill the vacant position. Although it was evident that he struggled to continue with his technical responsibilities as well as his newly acquired administrative and managerial responsibilities, management believed it was just a matter of time for him to get used to managing it all. They assumed he would learn his new responsibilities as he "practiced" on the job, and would "tell him" what to do. Now, with direct reports he had never had before, Steve's work began to fail on every level by the third or fourth month. Not only did he struggle as he managed others at work, but also in completing his own work. Management became frustrated with Steve and hardly realized it was they who had set up the young, pleasant, and driven employee for failure...
"

Assessment

In this quadrant, the individual is healthy, or has medical issues under control. The individual either does not perform or produce, or performs poorly. This may be a young and/or new employee, and/or an employee that may not have been placed in the best position at the job. As in this example, the individual may perform on a high level within a certain area (Steve would probably have been on IQ3 had he continued his technical position), and on another level with another skill.

Strategies

Identify healthy strategies and continue to use them. The individual in this quadrant should seek for development and performance skills training. Consider increasing your knowledge with furthering training or education, seeking someone's coaching or mentoring, or getting career counseling. Establish specific goals to improve your situation. Maximize **The Four Pillars of Biological Health** and challenge yourself along the way.

1. Many people in IQ4 are young and healthy. Continue to maximize The Four Pillars of Health through exercise, good nutrition, good sleep hygiene, and daily relaxation. Avoid drinking in excess, and avoid caffeinated drinks to perform. Create long-term healthy habits.

2. Speak with your boss and/or other managers in your organization. Ask them for feedback about the best skills you need in your new position. Ask them about what you should watch out for. Your candid approach will help your boss realize you are serious about improving in your new job.

3. Ask your boss questions about his or her expectations of you, and ask to meet weekly for mentoring. Ask for a coach if available. Although there are many skills we learn at the job, you may learn faster if you get expert advice along the way. Most good leaders enjoy helping their followers as much as they can.

4. Ask to "shadow" another very effective manager or worker so as to see and experience why they are high performers. Choose three to five managers that you admire and ask if you can accompany them throughout the day to see how they do what they do. You may look up to different managers for different skills.

5. Speak with human resources and ask about performance evaluations and expectations from managers. Ensure you are well prepared to deliver what's necessary in your new role. If you are now a manager, make sure you clearly

understand the policies and procedures within your organization.

6. Set up your own goals as they relate to your new position. Based on your feedback with your boss and other managers, establish your own development plan by setting up your goals and meeting deadlines.

7. Check with your company and inquire about internal or external training courses that could help you further develop the required skills for your position. Many larger companies have internal training systems or special arrangements with local or Internet-based colleges or universities.

8. Ask your boss for literature you could read to further improve the skills you need. Ask your colleagues about what literature or training courses were helpful when they started their work.

9. Check online courses, training software, or trade schools that could help you improve your required skills. Seek to pursue certifications or degrees that could further help you advance in your career.

10. Create a comprehensive plan and integrate your technical, managerial, and any other responsibilities. Lay out an action plan with goals to be achieved at specific deadlines. Look at your short- and long-term plans.

Figure 14: IQIV—High Health, Low P2

ASSESSMENT:
Healthy but performing poorly.

STRATEGIES:
Identify and continue to use successful strategies for health: exercise, nutrition, sleep, relaxation, development and performance skills training, further education.

Establish a plan for improvement.

IN SUMMARY: INDIVIDUAL HEALTH & WEALTH STRATEGIES

If you find yourself in:

Quadrant IQI: Low Health & Low P2

Implement medical strategies first to improve your lifestyle and health, and then implement business strategies.

1. Consult a physician. Make sure you have the right diagnosis for your medical condition.

2. Many people in this category have both physical and psychological problems related to chronic conditions.

3. Start treatment. Consider holistic interventions: medication management, if necessary, rehabilitation, physical therapy, and alternative interventions.

4. If you are not exercising, start some kind of exercise: increase your physical activity by walking every day and build it from there.

5. Eat healthy. Add vegetables and fruit to your diet. Avoid fried food and food with high caloric content. Add fish and olive oil to your diet.

6. After you are able to take better care of your physical health, focus on improving your work.

7. Talk to your boss or your partners and work on improving one aspect of your work at a time.

8. Work with others so as to improve your cross-collaboration.

9. Understand your physical limitations but continue to improve little by little.

10. Once you have noticed improvement in one area, start improving the next one. Seek feedback and continue to improve.

Quadrant IQII: Low Health & High P2

Implement medical strategies first to improve your lifestyle and health. Make these a priority.

1. Consult your physician and get a comprehensive physical examination as a baseline. Check your heart and brain health.
2. Reprioritize your work and integrate healthy habits in your hectic work world.
3. Cut down on caffeine and alcohol.
4. Avoid taking stimulants.
5. Start exercising 30 to 60 minutes a day with repetitive exercises (walking, jogging, cross-country skiing, rowing, or biking).
6. Eat three meals and three snacks every day.
7. Start to practice relaxation techniques regularly: meditation, guided imagery, or listening to music.
8. Sleep at least six hours every night.
9. Spend time with your family.
10. Take time off on weekends and every few weeks.

Quadrant IQIII: High Health & High P2

Identify healthy strategies and continue to use them to improve your health and wealth situation. Establish specific goals to continue to improve within each and every area.

1. Continue to maximize **The Four Pillars of Health** through exercise, good nutrition, good sleep hygiene, and daily relaxation. Try a cardiovascular exercise for 30 to 60 minutes and add weight training to increase your strength.
2. If you are about to undertake a new business or job opportunity—and this is the best quadrant in which to do this—add some weight training to your schedule.
3. Eat three meals and three snacks a day. Eat at the same time every day and start with breakfast or lunch as your main meal.

4. Ensure you sleep six to eight hours every night.

5. Practice relaxation techniques and continue to create effective transitions from home to work and from work to home or between intense and diverse activities. Call these your Power Breaks.

6. Check your current business plan and fine-tune for further growth.

7. Learn and develop a new skill that will help you feel well and/or that will help you in your job or business (a new language, learning technique, or musical instrument).

8. Expand your personal and business connections via joining a new business, a networking group, or professional organization.

9. Continue to cultivate your relationship with family and friends.

10. Contact your extended family or good friends you haven't called for a while.

Quadrant IQIV: High Health & Low P2

Identify healthy strategies and continue to implement them. Maximize your development and performance skills training. Consider seeking further training or education, seek for a coach or mentor, and consider career counseling.

1. Continue to maximize **The Four Pillars of Health** through exercise, good nutrition, good sleep hygiene, and daily relaxation.

2. Speak with your boss and/or other managers in your organization. Ask them for their feedback on the best skills needed in your new position and things to watch out for.

3. Ask your boss questions about his expectations of you, and ask to meet weekly for mentoring. Ask for a coach if available.

4. Ask to "shadow" another very effective manager or worker so as to see and experience why he or she is a high performer.

5. Speak with human resources and ask about performance evaluations and expectations from managers.

6. Set up your own goals as they relate to managing people.

7. Check with your company and inquire about internal or external training courses that could help you further develop the required skills for your position.

8. Ask your boss for literature that you could read to further improve the skills you need.

9. Check online courses, training software, or trade schools that could help you improve your required skills.

10. Create a comprehensive plan and integrate your technical, managerial, and any other responsibilities. Lay out an action plan with goals to be achieved at specific deadlines.

Figure 15: Individual Strategies

PERFORMANCE & PRODUCTIVITY	LOW HEALTH HIGH P2 **MEDICAL/ LIFESTYLE** **II**	HIGH HEALTH HIGH P2 **CONTINUOUS IMPROVEMENT** **III**
	I LOW HEALTH LOW P2 **MEDICAL/ BUSINESS**	**IV** HIGH HEALTH LOW P2 **BUSINESS/ EDUCATION**

THE HEALTH CONTINUUM

Interview 4

"Lead With Passion"
JANET VERGIS

Janet Vergis is the immediate past president of Janssen Pharmaceuticals (a division of Johnson & Johnson). Her strong leadership and tremendous passion for patients have guided her as she has helped her organizations successfully navigate a very competitive marketplace. Janet contributed to a number of Johnson & Johnson companies during her 21 years with the organization, holding a variety of positions in pharmaceutical research, new product development, sales, and marketing. She's now hard at work in a new entrepreneurial venture.

JANET VERGIS ON LEADING
UNDER PRESSURE

Vergis: When you get into a leadership position, I don't think there is a day that you don't feel pressure—a big part of that is the need to make tough decisions. If I think about the really tough decisions I've had to make, they usually fall into one of two categories: decisions [such that] not all the information is available or clear and there doesn't seem to be an obvious right or wrong, and decisions [such that] the answer is apparent, but the *implementation* is difficult. It takes courage to make both types of decisions. One of these that immediately comes to mind was when I had to downsize one of our divisions. The business need to do this was actually quite clear, but implementing that decision—one that had such a tremendous impact on employees—was extremely difficult.

Cora: *Is it human-related issues that made you feel that this was a situation of greater pressure?*

141

Absolutely. There was the obvious pressure of needing to make our business goals despite the fact that we would have less people and resources, but the bigger difficulty for me was the human toll. A downsizing impacts not only the people we have to let go, but also the people who are left as "survivors."

These are some of the hardest decisions leaders face. Did you do it alone? Did you take some of these decisions home and sleep on them? How did you make these choices?

Sure you can sleep on it—or, perhaps better characterized in my case, stay awake because of it, but for big decisions I always try to bring in the expertise of others. Good decisions can't be made in a vacuum. I strongly believe that divergent opinions and different perspectives will always lead to stronger decisions. In addition, the more people you can engage in being part of the decision, the easier it will ultimately be to implement.

How did your position evolve in terms of experiencing more pressure and taking on more responsibilities? Do you feel that there were some special capabilities or skills that you brought in that helped you?

I definitely have adapted to the increasing pressures over the years. If there was one particular characteristic that I think has helped me it would probably be my strong passion for the patients who need our help. I've found that no matter how difficult the decision or tough the business environment, keeping a clear focus on the people that benefit from our medicines—the patients and their families—has made my job much easier and certainly more rewarding.

Is there anything in particular that you would have predicted about yourself? Did you have any idea what kinds of responsibilities you were going to have along the way? Did you know what you were getting into?

I had no clue what I was getting into (which is likely a good thing), and never had any goal or desire to lead a multi–billion dollar organization. It's never been about the title or the position for me, but rather the incredible satisfaction I get from contributing to something that is really important—[someplace] where I can personally make a difference. So I suppose in that regard I have actively sought jobs that offered challenges and complexity, but I've also pursued roles where I knew I could surround myself with great people and enjoy the work I was doing.

Is there anything else that you would like to add that you feel is important to share with the readers, anything else that may have characterized your work?

It may sound obvious, but it's important that when you're going through any type of challenge not to lose sight of the big picture and your overall goal. Challenges and problems are not only stressful, but by their nature require additional focus, time, and energy. It's easy to become so focused on solving the problem at hand that you lose sight of the larger objective.

Was that a natural way for you to remain focused on that vision or did you cultivate that through time and through your different responsibilities?

It's easy to stay focused on meeting the end goal when your end goal involves helping people who suffer from mental illness. It's impossible not to be touched and motivated to help once you understand the overwhelming need. I very much believe that many, if not most Janssen employees share that passion and I would say that it's one of the main reasons why they do what they do.

Sounds like you have helped a lot of people. What came naturally to you may not have come as naturally to others. Are there any other things you've found to be helpful in implementing these kinds of communications? This one, for example, was what to do first so that everyone could be on the same page.

I always tried to share my passion by ensuring patient needs are discussed in all company communications. I would also frequently invite patients and/or caregivers to come to the company and share their real life stories of living with mental illness. The reception was always fantastic and the impact immeasurable. It reinforced and reinvigorated our focus and kept patients' best interest as a top priority.

In general, I'm of the mindset that it's almost impossible to over-communicate with your team. This becomes even more important during challenging times, times of change, and/or when any tough decision needs to be made. People will not always agree with the decisions of leadership but it is critical they understand *why* certain decisions are being made. The transparency and the frequency of communications are paramount in maintaining trust—particularly when the decisions are not popular.

And you will gain their respect for doing what you do for the right reasons.

That is the hope. It's also important to note that the communication must go both ways. You can't just say, "Okay, I've told you everything you need to know, I've been completely transparent, you should all be happy now." To engage people fully, it has to be a dialogue. It's easy to do with your direct reports and your staff—you can all meet in a room—but when you have several thousand employees, you need to make sure that you have multiple means to connect, such as town hall meetings, confidential surveys, conference calls, etc. What's most important however is to really listen to the input and feedback. The only thing worse than not asking for input is asking for it and then completely ignoring it. It's not to say that you won't still end up making the same decision, but people need to know their voice has been truly heard. That's important in order to come up with the best solution *and* to maintain the trust and respect of the organization.

In her recent role as president of Janssen, McNeil Pediatrics, and Ortho-McNeil Neurologics (CNS businesses for Johnson & Johnson), **Janet Vergis** led a $6 billion portfolio with more than 1,700 employees. Janet was appointed to the post of president of Janssen in 2004, assumed responsibility for Ortho-McNeil Neurologics in 2006, and McNeil Pediatrics in 2007. Janet contributed to a number of Johnson & Johnson companies during her 21 years with the organization, holding a variety of positions including worldwide vice-president for the Central Nervous System medicines business and vice-president of CNS sales and marketing at Janssen. Janet earned a bachelor's degree in biology and a master's degree in physiology at Penn State.

CHAPTER 5
INDIVIDUAL STRATEGIES TO IMPROVE PERFORMANCE, PRODUCTIVITY, HEALTH, AND WELL-BEING

The following concepts are simple, and yet, it is an art to align, integrate, and manage strategic planning. **Leading Under Pressure** offers effective strategies to improve each and every aspect of your health, focusing on maximizing your performance and productivity while experiencing health and well-being. *Managing Work in Life* provides additional ideas to integrate these strategies into a comprehensive plan bringing together a busy work-life and a rich life experience.

The nature of my work is to assess individual and organizational situations (performance and productivity improvement as well as critical situations) to diagnose areas that need to be fixed, to develop plans to improve, and to guide all key players to execute the plan and succeed through its completion. To simplify the overall strategy to improve health, performance, and productivity, I use the following concepts both in my wellness coaching programs and in my medical practice of integrative psychiatry. I call it "AIM I AM," and use this acronym in a constant improvement cycle. "AIM" stands for Align, Integrate, and Manage your plan; "I AM" stands for Improve, Achieve, and Maintain each targeted goal.

☑ AIM
  ✓ Align
  ✓ Integrate
  ✓ Manage your plan

☑ I AM
  ✓ Improve
  ✓ Achieve
  ✓ Maintain your goal

This is a typical situation: A successful executive or entrepreneur comes to see me as he or she may be experiencing high levels of stress. These executives may have been very successful in their business endeavors, and yet many feel as though it's never enough. Although they achieve their goals their degree of satisfaction does not seem to match their degree of achievement. Why would this be? What we believe we want may not be exactly what we *do* want. A good goal may inspire us to get things done, but pursuing one goal after the other may prevent us from enjoying having reached each goal in itself. It's important to focus on our accomplishment even for a split second. This will help us ground ourselves in the present instead of constantly focusing on the future. Taking some time in the here and now after achieving a goal is essential for the experience of joy and well-being. Although we may express our joy in a great party, the experience of joy, bliss, peace, wellness, and well-being is an internal process.

Let's start with "AIM": Align, Integrate, and Manage your plan. This is a brief introduction to this section, further described in *Managing Work in Life*. "AIM" works for individual and organizational plans. Through years of coaching clients, mentoring colleagues and employees, and helping patients, I have realized that the more people are deeply **aligned** on a personal and professional level, the happier and more effective they are in their lives. This alignment means consistency throughout all aspects of life. A person who is admired by others and is a role model talks the talk and walks the walk. You can see many people struggling with this lack of alignment in some much-publicized affairs: a married politician who appears to be ultra-conservative and relentless when cleaning up illegal transactions is then found to hire a woman for sex, regularly. Another person introduces himself as a strong family man and is then found to have had several affairs in tandem. A parent says he or she is worried about his or her teenager using drugs but allows the teenager to stay over at anybody's home. An executive states his marriage is important , but when his wife tells him she misses him, he continues to travel alone for months. An employer says life-work balance is important but makes unnecessary demands after hours. All of these are examples of lack of alignment. If you say health is important to you, are you making this a priority in your life? Are you willing to do what it takes to improve and maximize your health and well-being? If so, you would make sure to discard all unhealthy activities and build on the healthy ones.

Next, you **integrate** your plan in every aspect of your life. If your calendar used to show your business activities, it should now include your personal and individual strategies to achieve and sustain health and well-being. Exercise and meals are now included in your calendar, and you treat these appointments with the same relevance as you would approach a business appointment—no interruptions, as you have deemed your strategies to be a top priority in your life. It's your child's birthday or your wedding anniversary and you say you value your relationship with your child and with your spouse? Then invest your time, energy, and effort to support your valued decision and make it happen in your healthy schedule.

The **managing** component is a very dynamic process. You create a plan, bring it to action, align and integrate your individual and organizational plan, and you manage your plan as you go. Your plan should be tested at specific intervals and should not be carved in stone. Instead, its purpose is to provide for a tangible opportunity for continued growth and improvement. Your commitment to your plan is key; many plans don't work because, instead of being used as a blueprint, they are kept in a locked drawer. Check your plan, summarize it, and carry your plan summary with you. Account for unforeseen challenges and opportunities, and continue to use this plan as a solid foundation for what you do.

Keep these principles in mind prior to initiating any plan you want to implement, whether it is a contingency plan, a business plan, a financial plan, a plan for acquiring or merging companies, or a plan for becoming a global company.

Let's address the "I AM" component, now. Once again, "I" stands for **Improve**, "A" stands for **Achieve**, and "M" stands for **Maintain**. Let me offer a couple of examples: Let's start with an example to improve our state of health first. Let's say you know you need to exercise to improve your health and you haven't done this in a long time. Let's say you want to start a cardio-vascular exercise. You would start exercise from 0 (absence) to let's say, a 2 (improvement measured by two points up). What activities would you need to implement to go from a 0 to a 2? Well, you could start by walking around the block once every day (that may be a 1), or walking around the block as many times as necessary to walk for 10 minutes (that could be a 2). Once you have achieved this goal—that is, of walking for 10 minutes on a daily basis—you would maintain this habit for a week before increasing your exercise time. In summary, you improved your baseline (moving up two points from 0 to 2), achieved your goal (of walking for 10 minutes), and maintained it (by repeating it for a week) before trying to continue to improve. As an example, the scale would look like this:

- ☑ **10**: (ideal): 30 to 60 minutes of cardiovascular exercise every day (jogging, biking, running, swimming, or cross-country skiing). Regular additional exercise alternating weight training, outdoor activities, sports, dance, martial arts, yoga, Tai Chi, pilates, or other practices.

- ☑ **9**: 30 to 60 minutes of cardiovascular exercise every day. Occasional additional exercises including those mentioned in 10.

- ☑ **8**: 30 to 60 minutes of cardiovascular exercise at least five times a week. Occasional additional exercises.

- ☑ **7**: 30 minutes of cardiovascular exercise at least five times a week.

- ☑ **6**: 30 minutes of cardiovascular exercise at least four times a week.

☑ **5:** 30 minutes of cardiovascular exercise at least three times a week.

☑ **4:** 10 to 30 minutes of cardiovascular exercise at least twice a week.

☑ **3:** 10 minutes of cardiovascular exercise once or twice a week.

☑ **2:** 10 minutes of walking at least three times a week.

☑ **1:** Going around the block once a day.

☑ **0:** (absence): sedentary lifestyle, no exercise, no walking, almost no physical activity.

Now, let's address an example to improve your performance and productivity at work. Let's say you are answering every phone call and every e-mail as it comes. You feel overwhelmed, and, not only are you behind on returning messages, but you are also backed up in the bulk of your work—writing proposals, creating sales strategies, finishing presentations, or submitting grant applications. The quality of your work has suffered. To improve this situation, you are going from a 6 (as you may be able to finalize some projects, although not very efficiently) to an 8. How can you raise two points? Let's say you create a scale from 0 to 10, where 0 is the absence of any work getting done and 10 is the most efficient and ideal performance you could have. This situation may look like this:

☑ **10:** (ideal): I am able to finish all my work and meet all deadlines on time. I receive minimal feedback to improve my submitted work. I return all phone calls or e-mails within 24 hours. Even if I can't resolve the problem in 24 hours, I always send a message acknowledging receipt of the request and a timeline in which I will get the work done. I discard all unnecessary work right on the spot, prioritizing as things come.

☑ **9:** (almost ideal): I am able to finish all my work. I receive minimal feedback to improve. My performance is much appreciated by everyone. I tend to be harder on myself, but, overall, my work is excellent. I sometimes miss sending messages acknowledging receipt of requests but I know I have them and I'm on top of this.

☑ **8:** (very good): The quality of my work is very good. I meet deadlines and return messages when I can, but I always return them.

☑ **7:** (good): The quality of my work is good. I send out my projects when I finish them and I check them once. I sometimes get some corrections on my work and I will edit and resend. I do what's asked of me and I'm not interested in going beyond what's expected of me as I feel that slows me down. I am reliable and return messages, although it may take me a few days to respond.

☑ **6:** (okay): Work quality is okay and I return only important messages. I feel somewhat overwhelmed at times and this impacts on the quality of my work. When I submit my work it usually comes back for additional editing.

☑ **5:** Not too good, not too bad.

☑ **4:** (under-average work): I am usually delayed in my submissions and in returning e-mails. The quality of my work is below average and many say my work is sloppy.

☑ **3:** Some work.

☑ **2:** Poor work; some things get done.

☑ **1:** I do some things; occasionally, I will get fired.

☑ **0:** I don't get anything done; I will get fired.

You can establish each goal by setting your ideal goal (10), describing what that attribution means, breaking down each point with its description up to 0 (absence of the skill, for example). Next, you would identify your position within the scale. Once you know your baseline, the idea is to improve each section by one or two points. Improve your baseline, Achieve your goal, and Maintain the goal prior to continuing to improve. Continue this strategy until you achieve your ideal goal or situation.

STRATEGIES TO IMPROVE YOUR PERFORMANCE AND PRODUCTIVITY AT WORK

Strategy #1: Fix What Is Not Working in the Present

Starting something new is very appealing. And although this approach is excellent for growth, it is a dangerous step if the foundation is shaky. Would you build the second floor of a house that has an unstable base? Assess your present situation and fix anything that is not working well before you move on. A typical example is someone going on a diet and setting up a goal to lose 20 pounds in one month, not having dieted or exercised for years. Another example is someone striving to become the best salesman over the following month after being the worst for years. Although these overall goals are excellent, the timing is off, which will probably hinder your ability to succeed. Instead, try improving your situation by moving up one or two points within each area, fixing what's not working first before improving to master each area on a higher level.

Understanding your current situation, both at home and at work and in each and every aspect of your life is essential for establishing exactly where you are and where you want to be in the next month, six months, year, or years from now. Going with the flow may bring some unexpected blessings, but leaving our lives to fate is like sailing without a compass.

So what is this decision-making process about? Should we assess each moment of our lives and become robotic players in the major game? When we can establish an efficient system for activities that are repetitive, we become free to create new ideas, grow our business, start projects, and resolve immediate crises as they arise. Part of this assessment includes checking on our personal, professional, and organizational strengths and weaknesses, opportunities and challenges, as we take the next steps to continue to grow. As the chess-player makes sure to have a board and all

153

the pieces in the right place prior to a match, so you must account for your tools, including all the critical parts—capabilities and skills—that will enable you to effectively play the business game at the highest level, and succeed.

Chances are you are the ever-accomplishing juggler, taking on more and more responsibilities at work and at home, wanting it all and not giving anything up. We still haven't figured out how to stretch our work days beyond 24 hours, but that time may come. Imagine having a week of five days of...let me do the math...33 hours each, and we could have a free half-day per week.... The bottom line is: Think about how you can integrate all those "must-do" activities with "may do" and "would like to do" actions, as you are, indeed, trying to do it all and succeed at each and every level of your life.

As an integral part of your strategic planning, you will need to identify how you spend most of your time and how you perceive most of your activities.

- ☑ **Must-do activities** are those activities that only you can do—only you can be the spouse, only you can be the mother or father, son or daughter, only you can be the business owner, manager, or employee. I continuously see people falling into the trap of perceiving *all* their activities within this area, taking away other options or opportunities. **Common traps:** leaving little, if any time for you.

- ☑ **May-do activities** are those activities in which you *do* have a choice; you may decide whether or not the action needs to take place, and you can also decide whether only you can execute the activity, or whether you can have someone else perform this activity. This is the area most people need to work on: It is essential to identify delegating opportunities in this area. **Common traps:** not delegating anything, or staying in limbo, not doing anything at all.

- ☑ **Would-like-to-do activities** are activities we desire and choose to do. **Common traps:** overindulgence.

Strategy #2: Establish Your Goals

Fixing something that doesn't work is a goal in and of itself. Once it is fixed, you are now free to continue to improve other areas. Is your goal to increase your productivity? By how much? Measure it in work/hours or return on investment. Do you want to go to each and every networking event in town? What's your goal? How are you going to measure your success? Why is setting up this goal so important? If you had time to target one goal, which of the three or more choices would you make?

How can we simplify the decision-making process of what goals to establish? We need to prioritize our needs and wants prior to setting up the goals we want to achieve. There are many ways to decide this. One is to identify the positives and the negatives of each activity you are about to undertake. If you want to go from point A to point E, I would suggest that you look into the **positives (pros)** or **negatives (cons)** of going through each step first. Let's say you have three job offers in three similar but not identical positions in three very different cities. Grab three sheets of paper, and designate one job opportunity to each page. Write all the pros and cons of each of the positions. Next, do the same with each city. What next? Cross match: Let's say you love one job offer but hate the job, and you hate one job but love the city. How would you make a decision? Is it more important for you to have a great job or to live in a great city? All these questions and answers will help you make somewhat complex decisions. Once you decide what you want to do, the rest of the plan becomes much easier.

When making health decisions, we sometimes struggle with what to do first, second, and third. Many times, people give up before trying. Let's say you are struggling with newly diagnosed type 2 diabetes and hypertension. You have put on some extra pounds throughout the years, you have a strong family history of both conditions, you don't exercise, you smoke, and you drink in excess. A good healthcare practitioner will suggest you need to lose weight, start exercising, start a diet, stop smoking, and stop drinking, but he or she will also guide you as to what to do first

155

and what takes priority. He or she may ask you to take several small steps that will improve all of these situations, and will hopefully also guide you regarding how to do this.

Once you decide your priorities, it is then appropriate to establish a path toward reaching your well-thought-out goals. You may also look into performing a **SWOT analysis**, looking at the Strengths, Weaknesses, Opportunities, and Threats of each major endeavor you are to undertake. Let's say your goal is to lose weight. Your strengths may include being determined, strong-willed, and driven to do this; your weakness may be having a sweet tooth; your opportunities may be hiring a trainer and nutritionist; and your threats may be going on a business trip where you tend to have eating excesses.

Smart Goals, first described by Locke and Latham in their motivational theory and modified throughout time with practical add-ons, include the need for goals to be specific, measurable, and motivating; achievable and attainable; realistic and relevant; tangible and traceable through time. You can easily apply this strategic approach when improving and striving to achieve a higher level in your work performance and productivity as well as in your health and well-being. Let's use the same example: you want to lose weight. How do you make this goal specific? By saying you want to start from your present weight (220) and get down to 180. You need to lose 40 pounds in six months, and you want to lose eight pounds in the next month. You break this goal down in two pounds per week. Losing two pounds per week for the first month is possible in your mind, and very relevant given your needs. You will track your progress by creating a spreadsheet, writing the date and the loss in pounds or kilos.

Strategy #3: Prioritize Your Daily Schedule

Many people are so busy these days they don't feel they have time or energy to prioritize daily activities. And yet, when we are able to prioritize our activities we become more effective, more efficient, and able to free our time to do those things that only we can do. Here are some tips that will help you prioritize your schedule:

1. Plan your work in life, particularly what is routine.

2. Create a schedule and stick to it.

3. Keep a master calendar. Anticipate areas in which you may add activities. Avoid double- or triple-booking (redundant, isn't it?).

4. Organize and plan all regular assignments and activities ahead of time. Include them in your calendar.

5. When someone asks you if you can participate in a project or start a new one, before voicing a yes without thought, suggest you will need to check your calendar and get back to them. This will give you the opportunity to see how much time you really have for this new project. If you must do it, it will help you decide when as you compare what takes priority over the other.

6. If your boss tells you all three (for example) projects are equally important, ask which one he or she wants you to do first, second, and third.

7. Cross-collaborate: see if others are involved in similar projects and see how you can work together by distributing the work.

8. Designate specific notebooks for specific projects. Keep an organized outline.

9. Write your ideas or "to do" in the Notes section on your handheld, BlackBerry, or iPhone.

10. Meet with your staff regularly with the goal of establishing effective strategies to achieve your goals and become more efficient.

11. Avoid unnecessary interruptions while you work. If you are pressured by a deadline as you prepare a report, avoid answering e-mails or calls that will distract your full attention and delay the completion of your project. If you feel the need to "multitask" for distraction, listen to music while you work.

12. Use checklists, particularly if you feel inundated by multiple requests. Work in threes; complete and check the

first three activities you need to do by order of priority, and then move on to the next three.

13. Revise your list. Discard whatever has been repeatedly left on the back burner. If you haven't completed the activity for one year, decide whether it needs to be done at all. Delegate it if you still feel the action needs to take place, or delete it completely from your list if you decide it is no longer relevant. Let go: do not hold on to things you are not going to do. Create "good space" to allow good opportunities to come your way.

14. Start your morning with the most relevant work you need to complete. This may be initiating or returning business calls, sending reports, or resolving outstanding problems. Let's say you need to call five clients and you feel somewhat anxious about making these phone calls. Start by calling the client with whom you feel you have the best relationship, and then call the rest. Set up a specific amount of time for each phone call.

15. Write down the main points prior to the call so as to be prepared.

16. Prepare for the day or week ahead. This will provide for a good sense of being ready for the challenges.

17. Provide necessary support, mentoring, or coaching, or work with others. Delegate as needed.

18. Ensure your health is a priority bearing similar weight to any other business need.

19. Remember: you and your loved ones come first.

Strategy #4: Have Meetings That Work for You

Many executives and entrepreneurs feel swamped with endless meetings with no tangible outcome. Operating through meetings is not an efficient—or effective—strategy for getting things done. Although planning is an essential component that needs to take place prior to undertaking a given activity, micromanaging activities, or discussing processes forever won't necessarily ensure the final product will be any better than if you had just focused on achieving your goal directly. There are times to make executive decisions with advice from a select few, and there are other times to rule by consensus. If you are the boss, you can set up the style. Schedule your meetings regularly. If weekly, the meeting should probably not take more than an hour. Extraordinary meetings, strategic planning meetings, or development meetings should be scheduled and planned in advance. These can take hours or days. In general, all meetings should have the following three key components:

☑ **Beginning:** There should be a previously designated leader, coordinator, or moderator during each meeting. The agenda, with the purpose of the meeting, should be addressed in advance and should have been sent to each member at least a day prior to the meeting. Everyone should have read the agenda and supporting material prior to the meeting. As you organize the following one, the agenda for the next meeting should be included in the meeting summary.

☑ **Middle:** After addressing the key points to be discussed, all participants should have time to discuss each objective. Moderating meetings is an art. As a rule of thumb, though, if only challenges are brought up, you must also request that all group members suggest potential solutions. Having some tangible ways of addressing problem issues will leave everyone with a good sense of accomplishment, whereas discussing only the challenges will leave everyone feeling frustrated. Summarize at least three points for each objective that resulted from the discussion.

☑ **End:** Outline the conclusions, address the action items to be performed during the course of the week, establish timelines, and identify those responsible for completing each task. Summarize the meeting in the following format and provide the summary to all group members. Use this overall template:

- ✓ Meeting objectives (three to five).

- ✓ Discussion points: The same points as in the initial discussion, and any additional points brought up at the beginning of the meeting. Include up to three subpoints of the initial points for discussion.

- ✓ Conclusions, action items, and deadlines. Outline three objectives for the following meeting.

Strategy #5: Create Deadlines and Stick to the Timeline

Create a plan and lay it across time. Many companies spend thousands of dollars in a one-time event: a talk, a seminar, a workshop, or a consultation. Whereas an inspirational keynote may stand alone, a performance improvement or wellness program demands a combination of information and an action plan of implementation. If all you want to do is be able to check "done," uninterested in long-term benefits, then that one-time event may suffice. Instead, for any plan that requires some behavioral modification, whether you are starting a new diet, an exercise schedule, a relaxation exercise, an educational program, a development plan for an employee, or a master plan for yourself, consider the following general outline:

1. Define your goal and its specifics.
2. Create the plan with the ideal in mind.
3. Break it down into points to be achieved.
4. Include the check-up times on your calendar.
5. When starting a new plan, check it on a weekly basis for the first month on days 7, 14, 21, and 30.
6. Evaluate your improvement, fine tune, and continue.
7. After the 30th day, move on to a monthly planning mode at days 30, 60, and 90, if things are going well. If you still struggle, you need to continue the weekly schedule.

8. If the monthly check is going well, consider continuing with the monthly check for a full year.

9. When there is consistent improvement, then you can continue to check your progress every three to six months.

10. Continue yearly planning thereafter, particularly if everything is going well. Learn self-assessment strategies and plan ongoing improvement.

WEEKLY PLANNING: Days 7, 14, 21, 30
MONTHLY PLANNING: Days 30, 60, 90, 120, 150, 180, 210, 240, 270, 300, 330, and 360
YEARLY PLANNING: Yearly thereafter

Strategy #6: Start a New Project

So now, you have a great idea! This is perfect if you are in Quadrant III: High Health and High Performance and Productivity. As you are busy in your other thousand chores and responsibilities, you start building a new world in your mind's eye. Your vision becomes stronger and stronger and you feel the thrill of this thought. The thoughts and feelings are also felt as energy in your body. You feel the rush of creation manifesting on the physical dimension at its best. The more you think about your idea (intellectual dimension), the more energized you are (physical dimension). The more energized you are, the more enthusiastic you feel (emotional dimension). The more enthusiastic you feel, the more you bring it all together, the more you feel how this idea will bring greatness to this world (spiritual and social dimensions). You have just created a new possibility, and it is up to you to bring it from your mind's eye into the physical world.

Wouldn't it be great if we were able to create and execute one idea at a time? Yet, a novel inspiration may prove itself dangerous in the life of the busy executive or entrepreneur. A new idea means days awake at night trying to continue all your other multiple and diverse responsibilities. You feel the pain of wishing to pursue your new idea and realizing things on your "to do" list are piling up. This great idea may become a thorn in the path of a hectic schedule unless you are able to have some sense of control of what's already ongoing. You start thinking of the positives and negatives of continuing things as they are versus implementing the new, great idea that you have just created. You have a zillion things to do and this idea is creeping up in your mind until you feel you are about to explode in a big bang of creation. The inevitable happens: You have decided to bring your willpower to its maximum power; you are ready to take this new venture head-on and make it happen.

This is a great opportunity to take a step back—a big step back—take a deep breath, and take a closer look at what your week really looks like. If you are efficient at keeping good track of your daily activities and responsibilities, take a closer look at your calendar. If you don't, grab pencil and paper and mark down everything that you do throughout the course of the day— **EVERYTHING**. This is your opportunity to check on how it is that you spend your day at work and at home. Once you have written it all down—meeting times, interactive times with clients, employees, colleagues, students, teachers, spouse, children, parents, siblings and friends, activities, and everything else—then lay out your "playing map" and see exactly where you stand in your maze of life. Aha! So, you *have* created a day with more hours, how could you possibly have been doing all of this, and how can you even think of squeezing in anything else? Think your new idea through, look at the pros and cons of carrying it through, and create your plan of action. Have fun with it!

EFFECTIVE STRATEGIES TO MANAGE CRISES

As successful business owners, managers, or employees, many of us feel as though we are in the "spinning 24/7 wheel." We wake up with a full schedule of things to do, at the same time that we juggle our own and our family's activities while working. This art may be mastered to the smallest detail until some unexpected event throws us off course. How do we continue conducting business as usual while dealing with a crisis? Regardless of where we live—hurricane-stricken areas, earthquake-prone ones, or man-made crisis areas—being prepared is essential to our survival and success. Unexpected events may be catastrophic in nature, but it is the emotional intensity that may overwhelm our senses (and good judgment) during those challenging times. Coping with personal loss, whether it is the loss of a close friend, a family member, a divorce, or financial difficulties, will add to the emotional turmoil while continuing to run business "as usual." The following are general, effective strategies I've found useful in my work as a consultant in crisis management, as a medical doctor, and in my own experience as a business owner. Although they could be tips within the crisis management part, they are also useful during calm times.

Strategy #7: Assess the Situation

If you are facing an unexpected event, whether it ranges from a catastrophic-like event to the loss of a significant family member or friend, ensure your own safety, your family's safety, and the safety of those who work with you. You cannot blink when choosing people first. Our thoughts are expressed into words and transformed into actions. Ensure that what you think and say matches your actions. If you believe there is an emergency and tell the world that you are in an emergency situation, and yet you continue other activities of less significance, what you are saying does not match what you are doing. Make sure your thoughts and words align with your behavior. Establish a "range of emergency situations," so as to react accordingly. Keep things in perspective: Look at the whole picture and avoid interpreting crises as overwhelming.

Strategy #8: Concentrate on the Here and Now

Take care of yourself on a regular basis. You will be able to respond to a crisis if you are in a good place to begin with.

Ground yourself. Find exactly where you stand during the critical moment. If you have a plan in place, go to it immediately and get everyone involved. Assign activities and actions to everyone and lead the way to resolving the situation assertively and steadily. If you do not have a plan in place, create a crisis team and work through the crisis together. Organize the discussions so as to resolve the problem together, take notes, and use them as a template for future planning.

Strategy #9: Go Back to Your Schedule or Plan as Soon as Possible

Start with the simplest routine; make sure your **Four Pillars of Biological Health** plan is in place. Break it down into small steps if needed. Go back to your business plan. This plan should be easily available, as, during times of crisis or personal loss (or both), it may be difficult to remember exactly what the next step was. Maintain a positive attitude about your ability to solve the situation. Look for opportunities to grow beyond just resolving the problem. Make relevant decisions that relate to your here and now. Move forward as you immerse yourself in change. Resisting it will slow down the flow, whereas sailing with inevitable change will bring about novel opportunities.

Strategy #10: Avoid Making Big Changes During Times of Crisis

Go through the critical thinking process to resolve the challenging situation. Avoid making drastic changes during the critical time. Many feel the temptation to make *all* the changes they may have fantasized about for some time. Take the time to conduct a quick assessment of positive or negative outcomes with each action you want to undertake. With more time, conduct a SWOT analysis: address the Strengths and Weaknesses, Opportunities and Threats of each further action.

Strategy #11: Approach Your Trusted Circle

Build your supportive network in times of peace. Many people have shared with me that they were not at their best intellectual ability during times of tremendous stress, and believe they made poor decisions they later regretted. Learn exactly what each of your employees, colleagues, and friends can offer. Some may offer their emotional support or be good listeners, and others may offer their advice and help you make decisions. Avoid isolating yourself, and allow yourself to collaborate with others who may also be going through a hard time. You'd be surprised how many people around you may be willing to help if you only ask.

Strategy #12: Establish Significant Relationships Beyond Your Comfort Group

Keep a tightly knit networking group. This strategy will assist you by providing support while striving for a swift recovery. Stay connected. This will allow you to be close to others who may share common goals and the need for collaboration, as well as create opportunities to sell products or services. Move toward your goals on an individual level and see how you can cross-collaborate with others to maximize everybody's benefit. Think about contacting three people you know on a daily basis as you are trying to bounce back from the critical situation.

Strategy #13: Assess Your Intervention

Evaluate what worked and what didn't work for you. Improve your overall plan, and plan ahead. Consider this an opportunity to continue to improve your business and to simplify as much of the process as possible. Many people expect a magic solution to resolve a time of crisis, but the most effective strategies still entail being consistently organized on a regular basis. Keep hope alive. As entrepreneurs leading your companies or executives leading and managing your work group, others will look up to you to lead them during times of crisis. This does not mean you have to do it all alone. Share your hope and concerns with others as you move forward. This sharing will not only inspire others but will also refuel your own energy as you move forward.

STRATEGIES TO IMPROVE YOUR HEALTH & WELL-BEING

Lessons Learned From the Healthy Individual and the Health & Wealth Matrix

1. The World Health Organization defines health as a state of complete physical, mental, and social well-being and not merely the absence of disease or infirmity.

2. Think of yourself as a core of dimensions in full alignment: physical, emotional, intellectual, social, and spiritual. Your ability to perform at your best within each dimension is measured by your performance and productivity within each dimension.

3. Set up regular times for all habits: waking or sleep time, relaxation, exercise, nutrition, work, reading, and watching television. You may be spontaneous in other activities, but ensure your core is intact no matter what. As these habits become routine, you won't even question whether or not to do them.

4. Create healthy habits and practice them daily. Be consistent.

5. Promote healthy habits in those around you. Lead by example. If you want a smoke-free campus, be the first to stop smoking.

6. Establish your baseline health and improve from there.

7. Establish your health priorities: Fix what needs to be resolved first, and then improve.

8. If you have to fix several areas, ask for help to establish which to do first, second, and third.

9. Create the 10-step health improvement scale and focus on the one area you are trying to fix and improve. Use Improve, Achieve, and Maintain as a model.

10. Spread out your timelines so that you can track your improvement.

166

Strategies to Improve Physical Health

Nutrition

11. Consider meals as sacred times. No working on the phone or the computer, and no multi-juggling. You are better off taking 10 to 15 minutes to be relaxed while you eat rather than taking 20 to 30 minutes for a constantly interrupted meal.

12. Have breakfast and dine with your family and children. Not only will they do better in school but you will have the opportunity to establish an exceptional relationship with them. Excellent relationships lead to mutual respect and further understanding of one another. If you are able to do this, there will be a slim chance of your not knowing your child when he or she becomes a teenager.

13. Make a list of your family's traditional food, particularly if your family members have lived long and healthy lives. If so, include family dishes in your daily menu.

14. Change unhealthy family habits if your family members were obese or experienced medical conditions such as high blood pressure, diabetes, and cancer.

15. Eat at least three meals a day.

16. Make either breakfast or lunch your main meal of the day. If you are awake 16 hours, spread eating to every four to six hours.

17. Eat three snacks in between meals.

18. Carry healthy snacks with you at all times (for example, a mix of dried berries and nuts). This is the fastest way of giving you an energy boost during a long day at work.

19. Avoid drinking more than two cups of coffee during the day or after two in the afternoon. Watch your caffeinated drink consumption.

20. If you love eating meat, ensure you also eat plenty of fruits and vegetables.

21. Add fish to your diet.

22. Avoid eating in the middle of the night.

23. Avoid "avoiding" food. If you are now binging carbohydrates (such as chocolate, cookies, or ice cream), eat your full meal first and have a measured portion of your favorites as dessert.

24. If you believe bariatric surgery will help you lose weight and maintain your new way on its own, think again. Long-term poor eating habits are not replaced by shrinking the stomach through this procedure. Instead, good behavior replaces bad behavior; good eating habits replace poor eating habits. Create positive eating habits even if you decide to have the surgery.

25. Make a list of the food you need before going to the supermarket.

26. Avoid going to the supermarket when you are hungry.

27. Eat at the same time every day.

28. Avoid eating right before exercising.

29. Try serving smaller portions for you and your family.

30. When dining out at all-you-can-eat restaurants, start with fruit and salads first.

31. Have vegetables and fruits with every meal.

32. Teach your kids healthy eating habits by setting the example.

33. You may take kids for an occasional treat, but avoid feeding them fast food daily.

34. Don't smoke.

35. Drink up to two glasses of wine or beer a day.

36. Avoid liquor or drink only one or two drinks in social gatherings.

37. Don't drink and drive.

38. Avoid drinking alcohol to sleep at night.

39. Avoid taking hypnotics (over-the-counter or prescribed) for more than two weeks.

40. Set your purpose: Choose to bring to your body only food and beverages that will be healthy for you. Avoid anything that is unhealthy for you.

Exercise

41. Exercise at least 30 minutes every day.

42. Practice a repetitive exercise daily: power walk, treadmill or elliptical, swimming, jogging, or rowing.

43. Listen to music and/or read while exercising.

44. Instead of reading gossip magazines, try reading highly complex material while you are on the treadmill or elliptical. Your increased blood flow—and lack of interruptions—will make it the perfect time to focus, concentrate, and pay attention to challenging reading.

45. Avoid being on the phone while on the treadmill: Your breathing pace is of essence to oxygenate your body while exercising. When you "talk and walk" you will not benefit as much as when you focus on your breathing while exercising.

46. Focus on your breathing when eating, exercising, relaxing, or while you are about to fall asleep.

47. Find electronic applications to help you train while on the treadmill.

48. Change your cardiovascular routine every once in a while or use alternating programs that you can set up on the treadmill.

49. Practice this schedule at least five times a week. If you are working more than 12 hours a day you will benefit from exercising at least one hour daily instead of the half hour.

50. Exercise with the right gear. Prepare your exercise clothes, water bottle, music, reading, and everything you need in an exercise bag or backpack.

51. Add weight training exercises to increase and improve your strength, particularly if you have a hectic travel schedule.

52. Avoid weight-related injuries by taking into consideration your fitness level and age.

53. Go for a power walk and listen to music or to an audio book to create a transition when you come from work and feel tired.

54. Exercise with an exercise buddy, friend, or family member if you have trouble working out alone.

55. The best exercise time is the morning. If you can't fit in exercise time in the morning, any time you can exercise will work.

56. If you exercise in the evening but then feel too activated and unable to sleep, instead, exercise in the morning.

57. If you are leading under pressure, exercising daily is the most effective, cheapest, and most rewarding activity to help you raise your energy level in a natural way.

58. If you are experiencing stress, anxiety, and depression, you will experience exercise's relaxing, anti-anxiety, and anti-depressant effects.

59. Sex offers a good way of increasing pleasurable experiences and is a good source of exercise. It may be great to enhance your relationship and intimacy with your loved one, and having sex will also add a remedy against stress.

60. If you haven't exercised in years, start by exercising five to 10 minutes a day and increase your exercise time by five to 10 minutes every week until you reach your ideal 30- to 60-minute workout.

Sleep

61. Set up a regular time to go to sleep every night.

62. Sleep six to eight hours every night.

63. Avoid taking naps during the day.

64. If you are extremely tired, take a 10- to 20-minute break, but avoid going to sleep in the middle of the day unless you are culturally used to doing this (siesta).

65. If you fly across meridians, try resting during the flight, and stay awake until it is time to sleep at your destination.

66. Avoid taking red-eyes on a regular basis. Instead, sleep overnight and return the following day.

67. Avoid drinking alcohol to fall asleep.

68. Avoid taking hypnotics or over-the-counter medications for more than 15 days to help you sleep.

69. If tossing and turning, try to stay as calm and relaxed as possible by doing deep breathing exercises, guided imagery, or listening to soft music.

70. Avoid doing anything that is "activating" prior to going to bed: Avoid watching television and the news, reading interesting material, or doing intense activities. Keep the bedroom for sleep and sex.

Relaxation

71. Practice relaxation techniques as a routine.

72. Create "transitions" between intense activities.

73. Take Power Breaks after intense activities to gain your energy back.

74. Listen to music when you travel—in the car, on the plane, on the train, or on the bus.

75. Learn relaxation techniques, including guided imagery.

76. Learn meditation techniques.

77. Practice repetitive cardiovascular exercises and experience "the zone."

78. Practice dance, yoga, Tai Chi, or Chi Gong.

79. Learn a new hobby, particularly if it is artistic.

80. Learn how to go from a "tense" to a "relaxed" state and ensure you have more "relaxed" than "tense" times throughout the course of your day.

Strategies to Improve Emotional Health

81. Assess your baseline state of emotional health. Is there one mood that prevails?

82. Establish your improvement scale starting with the least desirable (0) to your ideal state (10).

83. If the prevalent mood is negative (constant worrying or sadness), contact your primary doctor or have an evaluation by a psychiatrist or mental health professional.

84. If you have been feeling this way for months or years, please note that it may take you time to shift into a positive mood. The earlier you start, the easier it gets.

85. Remember, the use of some medications (such as interferon or beta blockers) may make you feel down. Antidepressant medications are also described as having a "dulling" effect. Some medications may give you a high and then a crash, impacting on your emotional health (for example, steroids, including sex hormones and corticosteroids).

86. Avoid alcohol, cocaine, and other drugs as they may also impact on your emotional health. Although you may first feel a high you will then feel their crashing effect afterward.

87. Make a list of all activities and interactions that bring you significant joy in life.

88. Make sure you include at least one significant interaction and one activity that bring high value to you every day.

89. Focus on the positive more than the negative. Focus on learning effective ways to do this more and more.

90. Learn to identify and control out-of-control emotions such as anger, temper tantrums, or being hysterical about everything. Learn positive ways to address your concerns while staying calm on the outside and on the inside.

91. Avoid being around people who are angry, have temper tantrums, or are hysterical about everything. Help them seek help.

92. Practice relaxation techniques, as they will impact directly on your emotional state, helping you become more centered, in balance, and calm at your core.

93. Hold the purpose of having an outstanding relationship with your spouse, children, family, and friends. If this is your ideal, strive to find positive ways to enjoy excellent relationships with everyone around you.

94. Have dinner with your spouse and children to enhance the opportunity to develop a positive, outstanding, and longstanding relationship with them.

95. Schedule joint activities that will be interesting for everyone, not just for you or for other family members. If you don't have any interests in common, take turns to accommodate everyone, trying to find the activities that most people like.

96. Avoid constantly criticizing others. This is not only detrimental to their emotional health, but, believe it or not, it is unhealthy for you too. Criticizing others only means you are having negative thoughts about them. Instead, think about their positive contribution.

97. If you find your mind going to negatives about people, activities, or projects, make an effort to find at least one positive attribute.

98. Practice having a positive attitude.

99. Be of service to others. If you see others in distress, be the first one to offer help.

100. Practice opening up to express your true feelings to your spouse, family, and friends. Take away your mask and feel more comfortable in your own skin so that your feelings on the inside are aligned with your actions on the outside.

Strategies to Improve Intellectual Health

101. Assess your baseline state of intellectual health.

102. Establish your improvement scale starting with the least desirable (0) to your ideal state (10).

103. Take the time to visualize your short- and long-term goals in life.

104. Are you a curious learner? Try new ways to do the things you used to do the same way over and over again.

105. Take Power Breaks: Take time to relax between intense intellectual activities.

106. Learn a new skill: a new computer program, a new language, or a new instrument.

107. Read articles or books that you would not normally read.

108. When reading articles or books, use integrative approaches to learning. Include summaries of the main points or a mind map.

109. Maximize your learning style. Is it visual, auditory, or kinesthetic? Try learning through all styles: read the material, listen to its audio-book, and process the learned material by summarizing it on paper or as a presentation. Ensure multiple styles for complex material.

110. Use these same integrative approaches when preparing presentations. Avoid giving presentations without preparing in advance.

111. Teach others what you have learned. This will seal your learning. Share your knowledge. This will seal your giving.

112. Use technology to enhance your work.

113. Challenge your memory: Keep your mind active through puzzles that include words, numbers, shapes, and logical problems to be resolved.

114. Stimulate all senses.

115. Taste new foods.
116. Learn about herbs and their different shapes, textures, and smell.
117. Increase the variety of the music you listen to.
118. Try another museum or museum section as compared to the one you always go to.
119. Try a new exercise.
120. Make learning one of your priorities.

Strategies to Improve Social Health

121. Assess your baseline state of social health.
122. Establish your improvement scale starting with the least desirable (0) to your ideal state (10).
123. Be an active participant in social events at work that go beyond your job description.
124. Participate in at least one committee, group, task force, or activity at work.
125. Show your interest in learning about your coworkers. Avoid talking about what you know about them with others unless they bring it up in conversation.
126. Avoid gossip and making negative comments about others.
127. Even if you are in a competitive environment, focus on your common purpose as you work with your coworkers toward a win-win situation in favor of your organization.
128. Avoid staying alone in your office all day. Mingle with others at different times of the day.
129. Become active in your community. Join the local chamber of commerce, church group, or other groups with common goals.
130. Join your professional association and become an active participant in one committee or project.

131. Join larger associations that would provide for a combination of social gatherings and learning opportunities, such as Entrepreneurs' Organization or the Women Presidents' Organization if you are an entrepreneur.

132. Attend local, regional, or national networking events that support your overall plan.

133. Avoid joining too many groups or going to too many networking events. You are better off creating strong relationships with fewer people than having many superficial interactions.

134. Create strong relationships with a trusted group of colleagues and meet regularly.

135. Prioritize your meetings and attend the ones with the highest business or professional priority consistently.

136. Maximize your use of social media but avoid being addicted to it.

137. Use social media strategically. LinkedIn may be an excellent opportunity to connect with high-quality business individuals, whereas Facebook and Twitter may offer excellent ways to launch global projects.

138. Increase your connection with your audience in the era of technology: Write articles, newsletters, and blogs. Interact with your audience.

139. Learn about different cultures and the ways they relate. Travel outside of your comfort zone, out of state, and out of the country to expand your horizons.

140. Make social health a priority to connect with others beyond your circle of family and friends.

Strategies to Improve Spiritual Health

141. Assess your baseline state of spiritual health.

142. Establish your improvement scale starting from 0 to 10 (ideal state such as experiencing The Power of Wellbeing).

143. Describe the values that are important to you. Make a list of five to 10 values.

144. Find your experiences in which these values are completely aligned and mark other instances in which you believe they are not. Focus on improving those that are not in alignment.

145. Avoid being around people who are constantly breaking the rules, people who don't seem to care about others but themselves, and people who are not aligned with your values. Without judging them, realize you disagree on what's important and essential to you.

146. Avoid judging others for their lifestyle choices, age, gender, race, social background, or level of education.

147. Avoid watching programs, listening to news, or doing anything that is not aligned with your values or spiritual source.

148. Include activities in which you contemplate art in each and every form: visual (painting), auditory (music), or performance (dance and opera), to name a few.

149. Start an artistic hobby: music (instrument or voice), painting, acting, or dancing.

150. Find actions, experiences, and interactions that inspire you to improve.

151. Volunteer for a cause that is dear to your heart.

152. Practice meditation techniques and/or pray regularly.

153. Connect with your spiritual source on your own or by joining groups with a common purpose.

154. Develop tolerance and respect for others' practice of finding their spiritual health.

155. Set up your goal of being in peace, in balance, and to feel well at your core.

156. Be of service to others without expecting anything in return.

157. Help others who are also striving to maximize their spiritual health.

158. Create businesses, job opportunities, and activities that will bring benefits to the world.

159. Live to leave a positive legacy for those to come: Contribute to making the world a better place for all.

160. Make your life purpose to discover, experience, and enjoy The Power of Wellbeing.

Figure 16: Write Your Own Healthy Strategies

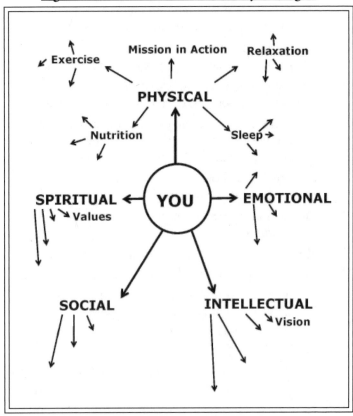

Interview 5

"From Firefighter to Strategic Leader" GERRY CZARNECKI

Through more than 40 years of experience as a leader, as a C-level and senior executive in Fortune 100 companies (such as IBM and Bank of America), privately held companies, closely held public companies, and large and small nonprofits, Gerry has been consistently committed to sharing his experience and vision. His enlightening management philosophy has led to the writing of several publications, including his latest book, *Lead With Love*, published in April 2010.

GERRY CZARNECKI ON LEADING UNDER PRESSURE

Czarnecki: Probably 85 to 90 percent of the assignments I've had in leadership have been a crisis or a stressful situation. So much of what I've done is going into something that's broken and fixing it. First, going into a troubled situation where there is a great deal of stress, where things are broken, where I mean literally that things are not working right; where either the company is working its way to bankruptcy or someone is in an operational nightmare that nobody thought they could get out of. The first thing that happens to the person when they take on that assignment, I don't care *what* they tell you, the first thing that happens is you get scared. You walk in and you find out either from the person that assigns you or from you taking the job; you sit there and say, "Oh boy, this is a serious problem and I have confidence in myself but I'm sorry, this has got me scared." Anybody who denies that they've got fear hitting them first is pulling the wool over their own eyes.

179

The second thing that happens once you have accepted the fear—because you have to accept it, it's a reality, it *is* there—you then have to say, depending on your options, "Is this the one I want to take on?" So first you have to accept the fear but then you have to ask yourself, "Is this one I'm prepared to take on?" I had a couple circumstances in which I had a choice. During the first 11 or 12 years of my working career and business, I really didn't feel like I had a choice. My boss looked at me and said, "I got this job over here, you need to go do it." And if I'd said, "Well, gee, I don't think I want to do that," I think I probably would have put my career at risk. Interestingly enough, the first time I went into a serious firefight, I was about three or four years into my career. I was being promoted into an operating general manager [position] of a big part of the business and it was a spectacularly big jump from where I was. It was announced that I would take over this function in about three months; there was a transition plan.

About one month into that three months, my boss came to me and said, "You know that big promotion I was about to give you? You're not going to get it. Because there's this little fire over here, down in a smaller piece of the organization and it's turning into a blaze and you need to go fix it for me." I clearly did not want to go fight that fire. I had this huge job over here, which was going to be incredibly fun in terms of it [being] a stable organization; it was one that clearly I felt that I had earned my way into, and I had cleaned up some other stuff along the way, but I had not taken on a blazing fire. Well, I ended up getting sent over to that blazing fire, with great anxiety about whether I should take it on or not, but I went in there and it *was* a disaster. Once I got over and accepted the fear part that I named, the second piece was that I had to step back and say, "I'd better figure out what's really going on here." Quickly after I passed this "I'm really anxious and nervous" part, I ended up having to drill down and really learn it.

One of the biggest blunders I ever had was that job that I just mentioned, where we created an elegant system to be able to fix the problem. It was spectacularly elegant. The problem is that

180

we attempted to implement it too quickly and without the right leadership in place. And it blew up. The first shot at it blew up. We did it overnight—in one night; we changed the entire process overnight—and the next day everyone came in and they had new jobs to do. And although we fooled ourselves into thinking we had trained everybody, the bottom line is we hadn't. People were not ready and we created more mess than we inherited. And it took me way too long to come around. It was a huge learning experience for me when I had discovered that I had ignored the number-one factor that was going to make the difference, and that is, "Are the people ready to execute? And did they have the leadership in place to do that?"

The first time that I got into the business of fixing a problem, I was the last man standing. This was within six months that I joined my first corporate position, and the organization that I was in had been very successful. And a number of the people who had brought that success were transferred out to other parts of the organization. The person who was put in charge of that organizational entity just before I got there simply wasn't up to the task. He could not pull it off. Within six months after I got there, the organization—the company—decided that he was not the right guy, but when they looked around, they had taken all of the people who'd had experience in that function out into other parts of the organization. And I was the closest thing to somebody who was worth betting on. And that was my first turnaround.

So I took it on and I fixed it and then about a year later, after I had fixed it, I got called on to do another one from that platform in the rest of the organization because I had done that. So now I had two, back to back, in a period of two years, things that I'll call "crisis management," and because I got them done and got them done successfully, I was cursed into doing them forever.

I remember somewhere around the 10th year of my world of business, I remember saying to myself, "Ah, jeez! How did I let this happen to me? Everybody else that I know is sitting in these soft, cushy jobs, having a big, good ol' time, and here I am working 12- to 15-hour days! This is ridiculous! What's wrong with me? I'm stupid. How did I get stuck in this path?" And I went on for a long period of time thinking I was cursed into ending up with these kinds of jobs. As it turns out, as time went on, I realized that I had been fortunate to have been thrust into those situations because they (1) capitalized on skills that I had, and (2) now, all of a sudden, there were people talking about change agents. And I realized I was one. I will say this: There are a lot of really good leaders who would *not* be good at firefighting. And there are a lot of good firefighters who would not be good leaders in organization—beyond the fire. And I was probably one of them during my early days. When you act quickly, you end up not doing as much consensus management as you might like.

When you are making judgments on the fly, once in a while (like in that case where I came up with the elegant solution) you just plain blow it. You do it the wrong way and it doesn't work. But that then means that you have to be prepared to say, "You know what, I screwed up! We've got to flip it. Can't do it that way." And people will say to you, "Well, I told you that you shouldn't have done it." "Yeah, I know. But it's too late now. We did it and now we have to fix it."

Gerry Czarnecki is president and CEO of O2 Media. He's the cofounder of The National Leadership Institute (NLI), chairman of the National Association of Corporate Directors (NACD) Florida Chapter, and chairman and CEO of The Deltennium Group. Gerry also serves as a member of the Board of Directors of State Farm Insurance Company and Del Global Technology, Inc., and is chairman of the Audit Committee of each company. He is a member of the Board of Directors of State Farm Bank and State Farm Fire & Casualty, and Chairman of the Board of Aftersoft, Inc. He is also a member of the advisory board for Private Capital, Inc.

CHAPTER 6

THE HEALTHY ORGANIZATION

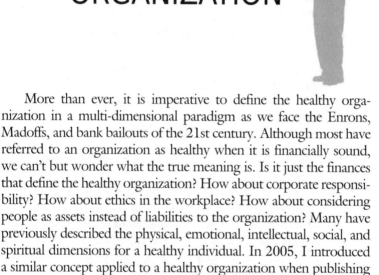

More than ever, it is imperative to define the healthy organization in a multi-dimensional paradigm as we face the Enrons, Madoffs, and bank bailouts of the 21st century. Although most have referred to an organization as healthy when it is financially sound, we can't but wonder what the true meaning is. Is it just the finances that define the healthy organization? How about corporate responsibility? How about ethics in the workplace? How about considering people as assets instead of liabilities to the organization? Many have previously described the physical, emotional, intellectual, social, and spiritual dimensions for a healthy individual. In 2005, I introduced a similar concept applied to a healthy organization when publishing the first edition of **Leading Under Pressure**. Just as we described all dimensions that make an individual healthy, we can define each dimension within the healthy organization:

1. **Physical:** The organizational body.
    Within the physical dimension we would include the safety, the structure, and the human element we choose for our organization. Whether it's our business or a multinational corporation, tangible financial health would lie within this concrete section. This dimension is also where the organizational **mission-in-action** is brought to life.

2. **Emotional:** The organizational feelings or emotions.
    The emotional dimension of a healthy organization includes the corporate culture—openness and trust, the

willingness to receive feedback to improve, and the ability to sustain employee hope during critical times.

3. **Cognitive:** The organizational mind or intellect.
   The intellectual dimension within an organization includes the training, the ideas and innovation, the learning, and the skills training necessary to constantly improve within the organization. This is where the **vision** for the organization is created.

4. **Social and Community:** The organization and its interaction with other organizations.
   The social dimension includes the interaction of an organization within a community and the relationship that it creates with other corporations, cultures, and organizations. This dimension exemplifies how the organization relates to the rest of the world.

5. **Spiritual:** The organizational values, ethics, and deeds for the greater good.
   In the spiritual dimension, the healthy organization's values compose the foundation of the organization. Ethical values, volunteerism, and altruism are key components within this area at the organizational level.

As in the individual healthy lifestyle, all of these dimensions are intimately related and interact in dynamic processes. Significant lack in one dimension will inevitably impact upon other dimensions. Let's say a company hires traders who will do whatever it takes to make a profit (physical dimension). This lack of ethical values (spiritual dimension) will affect other workers who may stay—or leave—because of the impact they will experience on an emotional level. Many will experience the intellectual challenge, whereas others will be shut down by the thought of using spineless strategies to succeed. The more people are hired, the more the company culture (emotional dimension) will be impacted upon. This will further influence the connection of this company as it relates to others (social dimension). As other companies, governments, and organizations observe its pattern of behavior, they may—or may not—decide to relate or conduct business with it.

On a positive note, consider SAS, the world's leading business analytics vendor and its CEO, Jim Goodnight, as one of the best examples of a healthy organization. On an operational and profit-based level (physical dimension), the company had a solid financial return while it reinvested 22 percent of 2008 revenues in research and development (intellectual dimension). CEO Goodnight propelled an in-house machinery such that he directly invests in his employees' and their families' health and wellness (spiritual dimension), understanding that, when well, we are able to produce and perform at our highest level. His appreciation is returned by tenfold in his employees' emotional well-being as they can freely focus on doing their part of the work, because most of their day-to-day needs are taken care of. On a social level, this is a role model that other companies, corporations, and organizations look up to as well.

Figure 17: The Healthy Organization—Dimensions

Physical	Saftey, structure, human element, MISSION IN ACTION
Emotional	Corporate culture, openness, trust, feedback
Cognitive	Training, constant learning, skills training, VISION
Social	Community involvement, relationship with environment
Spiritual	Ethics, volunteerism, altruism, aesthetics, VALUES
Performance	Quality of product or services, self-assessment and feedback evaluation, and constant improvement
Productivity	Work output, wealth

THE PHYSICAL DIMENSION

The physical dimension for the organization includes the safe workplace and the structure and foundation of the business, starting from the building itself to each and every piece of furniture, equipment, or technology used to enhance the opportunity to perform at the job. The human element we choose as leaders, managers, and employees falls within this category as people compose the physical aspect within the organization. This is also the area where our organizational **mission in action** is brought to life. The physical dimension of the organization is what differentiates one organization from another—it's like its DNA. A healthy organization will thus be responsible for establishing a strong foundation, with a safe environment, so that its human power will be able to implement its purpose, its goals, and its mission into tangible reality. Operational systems, policies, and procedures fall within this category.

For example, if you want to lease or build a law or medical office, you will need to think of the location, and its accommodations, access, and surroundings. Next, you would design its organizational chart: Who is going to do what, and how is everyone going to interact? How will you use technology to forward your business? How will you integrate the system? Establishing your clients and vendors comes next. Everything that deals with the physical structure as well as the human resource component resides in this area.

Examples of the physical dimension:

- ☑ Building: structure and foundation.
- ☑ People: structure and foundation.
- ☑ Furniture.
- ☑ Finances.
- ☑ Operational processes and procedures.
- ☑ Organizational chart.
- ☑ Mission in action.
- ☑ IT: computers and software.
- ☑ Communications equipment.

THE EMOTIONAL DIMENSION

The emotional dimension of a healthy organization includes its "heart." The corporate culture element resides in this dimension: Is the culture open or closed? Is it formal or casual? Is it competitive or relaxed? Is it family-oriented or single-oriented? Are people expected to bring a positive attitude, or are people overtly critical? Do people across age, gender, color, and sexual orientation relate with one another, or are there isolated groups? What's the company's attitude toward customer service? One of the significant points regarding this dimension is how different it can be in multinational companies. An office in France will have a very different flavor compared to one in Angola, the United States, or Chile, even when they may all unite under the same umbrella of the mother company. This dimension hosts the organizational emotional response to times of stress or crisis as well as the ability to sustain employee hope during critical times.

Examples of the emotional dimension:

- ☑ Corporate culture and "personality."
- ☑ Attitude at work.
- ☑ Behavior toward one another.
- ☑ Customer service.
- ☑ Openness.
- ☑ Competition.
- ☑ Tolerance.
- ☑ Ability to resolve conflict or crises.
- ☑ Interconnectedness within the organization.
- ☑ Ability to connect with leadership.

THE COGNITIVE DIMENSION

The cognitive dimension of a healthy organization reflects its "mind." This dimension includes its appreciation of intellectual learning. Companies that value constant improvement with the latest in applied technology have strong scores within this dimension.

These companies usually provide their employees with multiple opportunities to learn. They motivate their employees with further training, they invest in their learning skills, and they seriously commit toward continuous improvement. This is where the **vision** for the organization is created. Many organizations will value previous experience at the job, whereas others will appreciate the intellectual ability of its employees. This area may be particularly important as new generations enter the workplace: Whereas Baby Boomers have been conscientious at their jobs, sometimes focusing on repetitive tasks as needed to get the job done, Generation Y's diligence demands constant and rapid intellectual stimulation. This may be a very interesting area to explore in the years to come.

Examples of the cognitive dimension:

- ☑ Knowledge.
- ☑ Intellectual ability.
- ☑ Skills training.
- ☑ Constant learning.
- ☑ Company vision.
- ☑ Motivation.
- ☑ Research and development.
- ☑ Appreciation of intellectual ability within the company.

THE SOCIAL DIMENSION

The individual's ability to connect with groups is equivalent to an organization's ability to connect with other organizations. These groups include other companies—competitors, suppliers, and buyers—the government, the military, universities, associations, and other organizations at large. This area is particularly significant in the globalization of offering goods and services, and one to become more critical to organizational success in the near future. The more connections these organizations establish, the more opportunities they will have to provide their products and services.

188

Examples of the social dimension:

☑ Interactions and relationships within the community.

☑ Interactions and relationships within the same industry.

☑ Interactions and relationships with competitive industries.

☑ Interactions and relationships with other institutions (educational, religious, military).

☑ Interactions and relationships with government.

☑ Interactions and relationships with other countries.

THE SPIRITUAL DIMENSION

The spiritual dimension for the healthy organization also has its value system at its core. These values will inherently include the organization's ethics and its ideals. This area is where the organization's standards for its operation are created and where the bar is set for its success. This is the area where employers and managers will seek for alignment with prospective employees. The more aligned an individual is with her or his organization, the better the opportunity for ultimate success and well-being for both. This dimension is intrinsically connected with the emotional dimension, as distress occurs particularly when there is a mismatch. This distress will reside in the spiritual dimension but will most likely express itself on the emotional field. Ethical misconduct problems lie in this area. Whereas a single transgression can be interpreted as extraordinary, well-reported wrongdoing (impacting on Sarbanes-Oxley, for example) clearly relates to this dimension, where individuals and organizations are aligned, and not necessarily in a positive—or legal—way.

Examples of the spiritual dimension:

☑ Values.

☑ Philanthropy.

☑ Volunteerism.

☑ Ethics.

☑ Aesthetics and the arts.

☑ Wellness and well-being.

☑ The greater good.

189

Figure 18: The Healthy Organization—Integration

INDIVIDUAL AND ORGANIZATIONAL ALIGNMENT

The closer the alignment across dimensions between an individual and his or her organization, the better their relationship, the better their match, the better their chance of maximizing performance and productivity, and achieving longstanding well-being. As an example, if you like to play by the rules and you strive to be recognized as the best for your hard work (spiritual dimension) and you apply to work at an organization where the one who cheats the most takes the bounty home, you will not have a good match.

190

If you are extremely independent and prefer to work alone (emotional dimension) and you are at a position where your success will be measured by your ability to work in teams, you may struggle. If you enjoy learning new things at your job and you like that brain stimulation (intellectual dimension) but your job demands consist of doing the same thing over and over again, your job will probably be temporary. If you enjoy physical activity more than intellectual activity and your job demands that you stay at your desk for hours, there will be a mismatch. If you strive to connect with your community, groups, and associations and your organization demands that you work behind the scenes, you won't be able to enjoy this opportunity even if you love the job description. This is **alignment** (AIM I AM: the first A stands for Alignment, I for Integrate, and M for Manage your Plan).

Figure 19: Individual & Organizational Alignment

INDIVIDUAL ⟷ ORGANIZATION

Physical ⟷	Physical
Emotional ⟷	Emotional
Cognitive ⟷	Cognitive
Social ⟷	Social
Spiritual ⟷	Spiritual
Performance ⟷	Performance
Productivity ⟷	Productivity

Interview 6

"Mastermind"
MARSHA FIRESTONE

A tireless mentor, Dr. Marsha Firestone assists women business owners around the world. She is founder and president of the Women Presidents' Organization for women whose businesses annually gross over two million dollars. The organization is currently operating 80 chapters nationwide and is expanding to other countries.

MARSHA FIRESTONE ON
LEADING UNDER PRESSURE

Firestone: I was working for the American Woman's Economic Development Corporation (starting in 1990) and I worked for them for five years. The CEO/president was leaving and they were looking for someone new to fill that position. I was the vice president of training and I loved the organization. I loved what it did, its mission—I really thought I found my ideal career. I was up for the presidency of AWEO. I proposed to the board that if they selected me, I would start an organization called the WPO. I thought there was a need in the marketplace for this organization and that I would bring it to AWEO. It would be for women who had already achieved a certain level of success. There was nothing for those women who had already climbed some of the mountain.

And they did *not* select me.

I was devastated. I really loved this organization. I had thought I'd found a home for myself. I went home when I found out I hadn't gotten it and I really cried. Then I had a lot of conversations with my "mentor," who was the woman who had founded the organization (Bea Fitzpatrick). The way I dealt with it was to process what had happened. We talked about it at length, to the point where my husband was really sick of me analyzing it over and over again, and I developed a plan to launch the WPO on my own.

Cora: *How long did it take you to bounce back?*

They had announced that this other woman had gotten the job in November and I left in December. My father was very sick in Alabama. I went to see him, and I spoke with my mentor Bea about the next steps.

It took about six months to a year. It wasn't immediate; it took some time. It took some time for me to regain my self-esteem and confidence. And it took some time for me to come up with a plan.

What my mentor said to me is: How can you make the best out of this situation? How do you make lemonade out of lemons? In this case, it was really true. How could I go on in a way that satisfied the pleasure that I got from the kind of job that I had in the women's business community? How could I achieve some of my goals even without being in AWEO?

How did you deal with relationships through the transition?

I didn't stay there; I resigned. By the end of December, I left. There was this perception of the woman who became the president, and she knew that I had been one of the serious candidates, and I just knew I couldn't stay there, that there would be conflict. Ultimately, sadly—and I would not like to point the finger at her—the organization *did* fold. And I think it was the prelude (her leadership) that led to that.

As an observing expert, what do you believe may have led to that company folding?

There were more competitive programs coming out. When the company first started, there was no one like them. Throughout the years, more and more programs were developed to compete with it; less dollars to support it. And the leadership was not the leadership that it needed.

While you were going through the selection process, do you feel that you had an opportunity to be selected to that position?

Now that I really understand it, I think I was second or third choice. After the fact, I was probably second—which is what I heard via the grapevine. While going through it, I think I had a real shot at it.

Do you think you would have been selected?

What led to this other person getting it was that she was recommended by someone else. AWEO had someone on the board who had a connection to her and recommended her. There was a connection there—I could not have provided the same kind of connection.

Is there anything you want to add or share?

The lesson I learned is I didn't get what I thought I wanted. And so, I went out and did it myself, and things turned out better for me that way. And sometimes fate gets in the way, and who knows, it may ultimately be a better decision for you.

I did learn that and it taught me to be a little more patient when things don't go my way. Not *that* patient. But more patient.

The main lesson? Pick yourself up, dust yourself off, and move ahead; don't dwell on the devastation; keep going. Also, I think having my mentor to talk it through with or having a peer group (WPO) to help you with the next step, is extremely helpful to moving ahead.

––––––––

Dr. Marsha Firestone is the founder and president of the Women Presidents' Organization (WPO), which began in 1997 as a peer advisory organization for women who own multi-million dollar businesses. She is also the founder and president of the Women Presidents' Educational Organization, dedicated to increasing access to business opportunities for women's business enterprises (WBEs). Dr. Firestone previously served as vice president of Women Incorporated and as vice president of Training and Counseling at the American Woman's Economic Development Corporation (AWED).

Dr. Firestone is the author of *The Busy Woman's Guide to Successful Self-Employment* and has published research in business and educational journals on adult learning theory, nonverbal communication, and managerial competency. Dr. Firestone shares her professional knowledge by serving on numerous boards and advisory councils, including Women's Leadership Initiative at the John F. Kennedy School of Government at Harvard University, the Women's Business Enterprise National Council (WBENC), Enterprising Women Advisory Board, Forbes Executive Women's Board, Newcomb College Institute Director's Advisory Council, the International Women's Forum, and The Women's Jewelry Association. She also sits on Mayor Bloomberg's Commission on MWBEs for New York City. Dr. Firestone earned a Master's degree in Communication from Teacher's College of New York and a PhD in Communication from Columbia University.

CHAPTER 7

HEALTH & WEALTH QUADRANTS FOR THE ORGANIZATION

We have introduced the concept of the multidimensional organization. We have addressed how integration and alignment are key components of the interrelation between the individual and organization's dimensions. It is time to assess your organizational level of health and your company's ability to produce wealth through its performance and productivity (P2). Just as with the individual, consider the following matrix: picture the x axis as one that describes your organization's health, a continuous line going from little health (0) to a state of total health and sense of well-being (10). On the y axis, consider performance and productivity as your ability to apply your skills and capabilities to a tangible output: your own ability to produce wealth. Although performance and productivity don't necessarily go "exactly" together, they are close to your organization's potential to create wealth. Your organization may produce wealth by an exchange of work (sale of goods or services) for money, assets, and investments. The more output your company or organization produces, the greater the return. The more efficient and effective the company becomes, the smaller the waste and greater the gain. Rank your organizational level of performance and productivity by attributing a 0 if performance and productivity are poor, all the way to a 10 if excellent.

These are the options:

☑ **Quadrant 1:** Low Health and Low Performance and Productivity (P2).

☑ **Quadrant 2:** Low Health and High P2.

☑ **Quadrant 3:** High Health and High P2.

☑ **Quadrant 4:** High Health and Low P2.

You can apply these concepts for the organization as a whole, or you may also do this exercise with subsections or departments within the organization. This exercise will allow you to first assess your current organizational situation in the health and wealth matrix. The more accurate the assessment, the easier it will be to create your plan of action and implement successful strategies to improve your health or your performance and productivity. Next, we will discuss effective strategies that you can apply depending on the quadrant where you are. Some of these strategies are specific to helping you improve health, and some are specific to helping you improve performance and productivity. Choose the strategies that best apply to your organization and implement them in your daily activities.

Figure 20: Organizational Quadrants

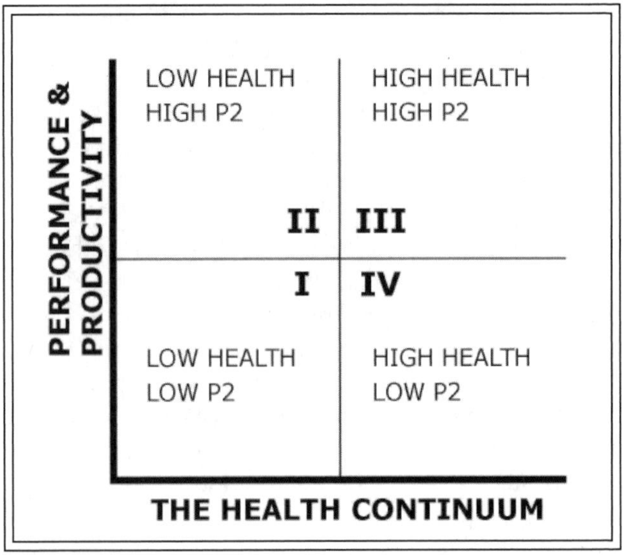

ORGANIZATIONAL QUADRANT I (OQI): LOW HEALTH, LOW P2

A nonprofit organization has recently been privatized. Processes and procedures that were in place are currently being revised. The merging culture is not aligned: There is chaos, expectations have shifted with the new management, and there is an underlying sense of animosity affecting employee morale, performance, and productivity. The old and the new cultures clash: Some say "the way we used to do it was better," whereas newly hired employees are determined to start fresh. The new leadership comes in strong, forcing the newcomers to be treated as the winners without facilitating a smooth transition. Employee dissatisfaction leads to turnover with a massive exodus.

Assessment

Similar to individuals, organizations in this category may be both acutely or chronically affected. This, in turn, will affect performance and productivity, thus impacting upon organizational wealth. These critical situations may bring significant change: The newcomers don't have much time to transition effectively but need to foresee transition needs so as to even out this process as much as possible. Many of the high performers in the previous organization may leave, whereas others will hold on to their jobs. A common mistake in these transitions is to put people to work (produce) without a sharing of vision or proper direction. This, in turn, increases tension rather than enhancing performance or productivity, ending in a vicious cycle. Instead, the focus should be on improving organizational health first and maximizing performance and productivity next. This organization may be experiencing high turnover and dissatisfaction in the workplace. Without proper leadership or a clear goal for everyone involved, this organization may experience high indices of absenteeism and chaos.

199

Strategies

Improve the organization's health first. Identify the areas with the most challenges, such as company structure, processes and procedures, and corporate culture. Make it a priority to inspire and motivate employees to work together for a common purpose. Fix other areas next. Coach and implement development skills after organizational health issues have improved. Implement the following key strategies for transitions.

1. Plan the transition before it takes place. This planning will enable you to anticipate some of the potential challenges and resolve these conflicts before they even happen.

2. Create a transition team. Include some of the stars from the previous organization and the strong players of the new organization. Establish very clear leadership with clear guidance regarding the new direction, but with a collaborative approach as you invite the new team.

3. Share the new vision with upper management. Have their buy-in. Invite them to share their concerns—if any—and then request their commitment to roll out your plan with their support. Once committed, avoid going back to continuing to discuss buy-in.

4. Share the new vision with all employees. Invite upper management as key players that will assist employees during the transition.

5. Promote a culture that appreciates what was good and worked well while being open to new opportunities that will help the organization continue to advance in a positive direction. Train your managers to invite workers to share some of their good experiences and invite them to also share some of what they would have liked to improve. Make this process highly interactive and positive at the same time.

6. Work with upper management to lay clear expectations and deadlines. Clarify performance and productivity goals and help workers shift into production mode.

7. Lay out these expectations with all employees through their managers at well-coordinated times from the top down. Create a reliable system that is somewhat homogeneous across the organization. Define the new corporate culture.

8. Facilitate access to resources and clarify policies and procedures. This will take a while, but ensure you have a plan in place. Direct your managers toward ensuring the significance of this process.

9. Evaluate the transition process. Be open to feedback to continue to improve. Avoid taking too long with "what is not anymore" and move on to positive feedback that will help continue to go in the right direction.

10. Continue to set up your expectations regarding productivity. Share the results of generated revenue and invite your employees to actively participate as an integral part of the process of success.

Figure 21: OQI—Low Health, Low P2

ASSESSMENT:

Acutely or chronically unhealthy.

Issues are not addressed.

Low performance and productivity.

Low wealth.

STRATEGIES:

Improve health first.

Organizational development & skills training next.

ORGANIZATIONAL QUADRANT II (OQII): LOW HEALTH, HIGH P2

This organization is a high-producing, top-notch, publically traded company. The company was originally

201

a pioneer, and it was well-known for its motto: The outcome justifies the means—any means. Gradually, although the company appears to continue to produce wealth like candy, back-stabbing and unethical competition prevails as the company culture. Companies that associate with this company have a similar adrenaline rush: Go for the kill for immediate reward. Employees who play by the rules exit fast. Everybody realizes that they must join the winners to stay in the game. Disgusted, some will stay in golden handcuffs as their lifestyles now "depend" on their income in this company. Even if their previous ethics don't match their current situation, many love the addictive feeling of living on edge. Others stay quietly while planning their transition out. And the winners take it all...

Assessment

Does this case ring a bell? Many observers seem fascinated by the loads of money piling in on trucks, whereas others are appalled at this unhealthy man-made scenario. Similarly to individuals, organizations in this category may be acutely affected first, and then, if the company survives, this will become a pervasive pattern. Many business owners, employers, and managers are reluctant to intervene at this stage. The illusion that wealth supersedes a healthy organization rather than understanding the relationship as a matrix makes this quadrant a tough one to overcome—not unlike the individual second quadrant. Stress, conflict, and friction will continue to increase, further splitting the corporate culture between heavy players and supporting staff. Sooner or later, this organization will consume itself and lead to its own demise. This situation is a time bomb.

Strategies

Improve the organization's health first. Identify each of the dimensions under stress and address those challenges first. Fix other areas next. Here are 10 more tips to help you improve your organization's health:

202

1. Come to terms with the short-lasting profit of an unhealthy organization. Some Ponzi schemes have gone on for years before becoming self-destructive.

2. Identify the key dimension at stake. Did you just have a massive lay-off and are now in charge of half the workforce you used to have (physical dimension)? Are your operations legal? Are they ethical (spiritual values)? Is your corporate culture cut-throat, ultracompetitive, and difficult for people to work together (emotional)? Do you reward only smart and gutsy employees (intellectual)? What is the company's relationship with other companies and organizations (social)? What is the short and long-term impact of this situation?

3. Assess the alignment between your individual dimensions and your organizational dimensions. Is there a partial or perfect match? Identify the mismatch and create a strategy to improve it.

4. If you are in charge of such an organization, realize you do have the power to change it. Set up your goal to make your organization healthier one step at a time.

5. If you are not in charge, decide to stay, change, or leave depending on your individual and organizational alignment.

6. How can you continue to improve the physical dimension? Improve the conditions at work, including a safe building and work environment. Ensure workstations offer everything needed to conduct proper work, and give access to adequate technology support and necessary equipment. Design the necessary human resource needs to conduct business.

7. How can you continue to improve the cognitive dimension? Offer opportunities to learn the skills to conduct business. Plan the intellectual skills required for your business: Do you need a good mix of younger and energetic workers who are driven to learn new skills on the job? Or do you need a seasoned workforce capable of

setting up their own goals and strategically deciding how to resolve upcoming challenges?

8. How can you continue to improve the emotional dimension? Define the corporate culture you want for your company. Is there tremendous stress with increased turnover? Are there violent and conflictive situations in the workplace? How are you helping resolve these challenges?

9. How can you continue to improve the social dimension? How is your organization interacting with other organizations? Are they having similar problems? What are the strengths of the connections and what are the challenges of sustaining these connections?

10. How can you continue to improve the spiritual dimension? Define your company values. Define your ethical standards and share these with the rest of the company. Ensure you have an excellent match between your individual and organizational values if you plan on staying with the company long-term.

Figure 22: OQII—Low Health, High P2

ASSESSMENT:
Acute or chronic lack of health.
Unaddressed problems.
High performance and productivity.
High wealth.
STRATEGIES:
Improve health.
Evaluate and fix problems.
Manage stress in the workplace.

ORGANIZATIONAL QUADRANT III (OQIII): HIGH HEALTH, HIGH P2

> *Everything is working well in this organization. The organization has just launched a new product and it was an immediate boom worldwide. This strategy was well thought-out with active participation from every team involved. Although there were some difficulties along the way, there was outstanding pre-planning and leadership while working together through the anticipated challenges. The company learned from a failed launch years before that resulted in a disaster with massive layoff and turnover. Looking ahead, it is preparing itself for some external difficulties that don't fully depend upon the organization itself. Although the launch sets up the tone for great growth, the company knows it cannot sit on its glory and needs to actively plan for what is to come. All teams are thriving; with an excellent attitude, they look up to their leader for guidance and they are proud of their own input in the overall process...*

Assessment

In this quadrant, the organization is healthy or has health-related issues under control. The organization maintains a high level of performance and productivity, thus having an excellent opportunity to build wealth.

Strategies

Identify the healthy strategies and continue to use them to continue your organizational health and wealth. Establish specific goals to continue to improve within each and every area. If your organization is in this quadrant, take the opportunity to grow, invest, and go to the next level. Implement new opportunities one at a time. Organizationally: people will be thriving with a great attitude in place. This is the perfect time to look at the "whole picture." Maximize productivity and efficiency: focus on one thing at a time. This is also a good time to continue to explore new opportunities, maintaining the acquired level of achievement before moving on to the next level. Here are 10 more tips to help make your organization perform at an even higher level:

1. Identify the key factors that contribute to your organizational health. Communicate your findings with your leading team, managers, and workforce.

2. Continue to look for any area that may need additional improvement, particularly if it affects your overall productivity.

3. Avoid "groupthink." An "everything is great" attitude, while good, may prevent seeing potential glitches in the system.

4. Be open to innovations and further growth. This is an excellent time to try something new in one area while everything is working like clockwork in other areas.

5. Plan your next steps. Anticipate potential difficulties and opportunities for the future.

6. Proactively look for new products, new services, new connections, and new opportunities.

7. Continue with a positive attitude and raise one challenge that you would like to overcome.

8. Invite feedback from your workforce to continue to improve. Keep the engine in constant movement.

9. Invite everyone to be a part of this success and honor their participation as integral members of the winning team.

10. Enjoy your success.

Figure 23: OQIII—High Health, High P2

ASSESSMENT:

Healthy organization.

Fixes issues as they arise.

High performance and productivity.

STRATEGIES:

Identify and continue to use successful strategies for health & wealth.

Establish goals to continue to improve in each area on an ongoing basis.

ORGANIZATIONAL QUADRANT IV (OQIV): HIGH HEALTH, LOW P2

This is a healthy organization. It has everything in place: a good structure, excellent people, and a great business plan. This young organization is breaking into a new niche, with big competitors in other areas, and yet there is still a well-defined new opportunity. There is some impatience in being able to break into the novel business, and, at the same time, everyone within the company knows they are on the right track and it is just a question of time to spread their wings and fly...

Assessment

In this quadrant, the organization is healthy or has health-related issues under control. The organization has a low level of performance and productivity, though, not producing enough wealth to sustain the operation. This may be a new organization, an organization in transition, or an organization undergoing drastic change.

Strategies

Identify healthy strategies and continue to implement them to continue your organizational health and grow your wealth. Review your business plan. Establish specific goals to improve productivity and performance. Identify immediate opportunities and execute a proactive plan to achieve the desired goals to increase productivity, performance, and wealth. The following 10 tips will help you in this process:

1. Assess your health. Check all dimensions and ensure you are not missing any deficiency in an area that's directly impacting on your performance and productivity.

2. Check your existing policies and procedures. Ensure everyone knows how to get from point A to point B. Make sure you simplify the overall purchasing process so that the buyer of products or services has easy access to the point of sale.

3. Create a clear business plan and lay it out across the company.

4. Focus on your marketing plan with clear short- and long-term strategies. Implement your immediate actions and track the results.

5. You may be the best new business in town but if people don't know you exist, you will go unnoticed. Ask your satisfied clients to write letters recommending your goods and services to their clients.

6. Integrate and align leadership and management efforts to offer clear direction of expectations to the workforce. Teach each business section to create goals that are aligned with the overall organizational goals. Guide the workforce to set up deadlines and ways in which every employee can check their improvement prior to reporting their progress to their manager.

7. Identify concrete steps to take and achieve as you focus on increasing performance and productivity as a means to building wealth.

8. If everyone is "hard at work" and yet not matching the expected outcome, evaluate areas in which you may be wasting what's coming in. Apply Six Sigma principles to your operation, whether it's goods- or services-oriented. Keep the quality of services when they involve people.

9. Identify companies that may co-promote with you and create strong alliances with them.

10. Focus on increasing your production of wealth. Spread your strategies across specific timelines: weeks, months, quarters, and years.

Figure 24: OQIV—High Health, Low P2

ASSESSMENT:
Healthy but performing poorly.
STRATEGIES:
Develop sound business plan and improve performance skills training.
Further education.
Establish a plan for improvement.

IN SUMMARY: ORGANIZATIONAL HEALTH & WEALTH STRATEGIES

If your organization is in:

Quadrant OQI: Low Health & Low P2

Improve the health within your organization first and then implement your business strategies to increase performance and productivity.

1. Plan the transition before it takes place.

2. Create a transition team.

3. Share the new organizational vision with upper management.

4. Share the new vision with all employees.

5. Promote a culture that appreciates what was good and worked well while being open to new opportunities that will help the organization continue to advance in a positive direction.

6. Work with upper management to lay clear expectations and deadlines.

7. Lay out these expectations with all employees through their managers at well-coordinated times from the top down. Define the new Corporate Culture.

8. Facilitate the access to resources and clarify policies and procedures.

9. Evaluate the transition process.

10. Continue to set up your expectations regarding productivity.

Quadrant OQII: Low Health & High P2

Improve the health within your organization first. Identify the dimensions with the most challenges first and attempt to fix those as a priority. Fix other dimensions next.

1. Come to terms with the short-lasting profit of an unhealthy organization.

2. Identify the key dimension at stake.

3. Assess the alignment between your individual dimensions and your organizational dimensions.

4. If you are in charge of such an organization, realize you do have the power to change it.

5. If you are not in charge, decide to stay, change, or leave depending on your individual and organizational alignment.

6. How can you continue to improve the physical dimension?

7. How can you continue to improve the cognitive dimension?

8. How can you continue to improve the emotional dimension?

9. How can you continue to improve the social dimension?

10. How can you continue to improve the spiritual dimension?

Quadrant OQIII: High Health & High P2

Identify the healthy strategies and continue to use them to continue your organizational health and wealth. Establish specific goals to continue to improve within each and every area. Take advantage of the opportunity to grow, invest, and go to the next level.

1. Identify the key factors that contribute to your organizational health.

2. Continue to look for any area that may need additional improvement, particularly if it affects your overall productivity.

3. Avoid "groupthink."

4. Be open to innovations and further growth. This is an excellent time to try something new.

5. Plan your next strategies.

6. Proactively look for new products, new services, new connections, and new opportunities.

7. Continue with a positive attitude and raise one challenge that you would like to overcome.

8. Invite feedback from your workforce to continue to improve.

9. Invite everyone to be a part of this success and honor their participation as integral members of the winning team.

10. Enjoy your success.

Quadrant OQIV: High Health & Low P2

Identify the healthy strategies and continue to use them to continue your organizational health. Establish specific goals to improve productivity and performance to increase wealth.

1. Assess your health.

2. Check your existing policies and procedures.

3. Create a clear business plan and lay it out across the company.

4. Focus on your marketing plan with clear short- and long-term strategies.

5. Ask your satisfied clients to write letters recommending your goods and services to their clients.

6. Integrate and align leadership and management efforts to offer clear direction of expectations to the workforce.

7. Identify concrete steps to take and achieve as you focus on increasing performance and productivity as a means to building wealth.

8. If everyone is "hard at work" and yet not matching the expected outcome, evaluate areas in which you may be wasting what's coming in.

9. Identify companies that may co-promote with you and create strong alliances with them.

10. Focus on increasing your production of wealth.

Figure 25: Organizational Strategies

PERFORMANCE & PRODUCTIVITY	LOW HEALTH HIGH P2 **IMPROVE HEALTH** II	HIGH HEALTH HIGH P2 **CONTINUOUS IMPROVEMENT** III
	I	IV
	LOW HEALTH LOW P2 **HEALTH/ BUSINESS**	HIGH HEALTH LOW P2 **BUSINESS/ EDUCATION**

THE HEALTH CONTINUUM

Interview 7

"Set Your Priorities"
LEYLANI CARDOSO

This savvy businesswoman and designer is both an international powerhouse and a mother of two, balancing these roles with class and style. This Cuban native founded Duty Free World International along with her mother and business partner. She wasted no time turning her business into a multi–million dollar company before hitting the five-year mark.

LEYLANI CARDOSO ON LEADING UNDER PRESSURE

Cardoso: Seven years ago, when my daughter had just been born we found out she had special needs. [At the same time], my company lost two major contracts simultaneously. I think back and to this day, [and] I say "Wow, those were really tough times." I think the first thing you feel is fear: for your stability, for your family. You have this huge responsibility. As a leader, you always feel that the responsibility is yours. How are you going to continue? For me, I allow myself to feel all those different feelings, and allow myself to accept that those feelings are normal. *Then* you can say, "What do I do?"

And then you start to take actions to try to deal with the situation at hand. You say, "Well, what do I have control over? I have control over how I handle things, what my attitude is. And what I do about the situation that is presented." At that point, it was a whole different ballgame because the company was concerned. We put our heads down and fortunately, we had a few months before the contracts expired and we were able to go out and successfully secure new business and eventually grow our company. The contracts that came later on were probably about

213

five times the size of the ones we started with. Even the process of obtaining the contracts was totally different, so there was a learning phase. All the while, we learned a new way of doing business that we didn't know before. At the end, we came out a stronger company, now able to negotiate on multiple levels.

On the personal level, talking to friends and talking to people really helped—realizing that when people are faced with challenges, they are faced with one of two options: they can mope about it and bear the weight of that, or they can try to make the most of the situation and make it a positive one. I've always had support, and a great support. But I feel that sometimes, no matter how much support [I] have, I've got to resolve things. I have this need to fix things and I have a "take the bull by the horns" approach.

Cora: *How did you end up creating new opportunities?*

"How did we get here? How did we end up depending so much on these companies?" And then you realize that if you make yourself a little more diverse and you're able to spread yourself out, you minimize your risk. So we started looking for ways to do that. Once we started doing that, we were able to turn that into a positive. But I think realizing what puts you into such a vulnerable position...sometimes, you're very involved in the day-to-day and you're involved in doing the things that present themselves to you, and you don't take the time to plan and prepare yourself.

How long did it take you to shift gears?

Generally, I first need that process of venting about it, and then, once I have it out of my system, I can move forward. It doesn't take more than a couple hours; at best, a day. With maturity, I've come to accept that I don't have to have an answer to a problem in five minutes. I feel that I afford myself the luxury of thinking things through a little longer. I feel that if the right answer is the right answer, it'll be the right answer tomorrow or in a couple of hours. Sometimes I think that if I put the problem aside and move on to something else, when I come back to it, I

214

may have a new perspective or the same perspective...and that's okay too.

I know that you work with your mother, so you have a family-run business. How does that work?

Fortunately, we think a lot alike in terms of our logic. Our styles of managing problems are different, but in the end, I think we agree on the core. It's a great balance because it allows us each to bring our own unique perspective. My approach is not necessarily better [than] hers, but combined it allows us the best of both. In my case, maybe I'm a little bit more aggressive because I'm younger; in her case, a little bit more astute because she's more experienced. That's how we approach things. In terms of having to learn a new style of growing the business or having to develop certain other strategies, [that] was fine for me. For her, seeing through all of that and coming up with a business logic and making sure that we were still holding true to the business model that had carried us all this time gave us a good formula.

You mentioned before some of the challenges you faced with your child. How did you make it a priority to be there for a child with special needs?

I decided to seek out the best possible help that I could. Sometimes that meant driving long distances, breast-feeding, and multitasking on my way to therapies. I dedicated certain hours of the day to prioritizing her needs and I knew that the second portion of my day, although not directly related to her, would ultimately benefit her so it gave me the sanity that I needed to step away and do what I needed to do. I also had the help of my husband, who shared the responsibilities and viewed it as a partnership, and took on half of the workload.

So you had the partnership with your mom at work and the partnership with your husband at home. What were some of the key points that were essential to you juggling it all?

I'm very efficient. I'm extremely efficient. If I'm driving somewhere, I'm not listening to the radio. I'm conducting a meeting, I'm making an appointment. I'm thinking. If I don't have anybody that I need to call or return a phone call to or anything I need to resolve, then I'm thinking about what I have to do. I'm prioritizing what I have to do. If I don't have anything that I have to have done, I'm thinking of what I'd like to do, what my next step should be, what I've done that I need to review. I constantly go through a reevaluation process, mentally. I'm constantly reevaluating everything that I do and trying to make sure I have everything in check. I'm very good at delegating. I check back with people to make sure they're still on target and I'll continue to move forward. Those are the key things that I do well.

How do you delegate?

I handle delegation differently depending on the task at hand. If I'm dealing with a publication or marketing, how I want to present my brand, I will sit down and review the concept but I will keep close tabs on how that is developing because it's very personal to me. I understand that even though I'm delegating, I need to continuously share and express my vision of the brand. If it is something that may not necessarily be as artistically inclined, but more cut-and-dried or straightforward, I will give somebody the project and ask how they would manage it. If I agree with them, great, if I don't, I'll ask why. I'll make sure that the main concept is there, that the focus is there. Provided that they have the skill set, I will allow them to do the task on their own. It depends on how closely involved I want to be on the project.

Do you have specific times to work and specific family times when you don't talk about work? Just enjoy family time?

We try to make family time separate only because we don't want to isolate other people that may be partaking with us and make them feel like they can't share, even though in the sense of our spouses—my dad, my husband—a lot of times they'll have good input as outside people looking in. But for the most part, it can get very dull for them if we talk about work often. So we try to make family time about something else. And we realize that we spend so much time together, we almost have to separate ourselves in order to grow on other levels.

Would you like to add anything else about leading under pressure?

I think that people who lead under pressure cannot allow themselves to be overwhelmed with everything that they have going on. I think that you have to deal with each crisis as it presents itself and know that what you're doing to resolve the issue at the time is the best that you can do, and to take it one step at a time.

One thing that I learned in regard to pressure is that you cannot assume what the outcome will be or let things get ahead of their course because sometimes it will take you into a panic mode or create a lot of added stress in addition to the stress you already have mounting. So you just have to deal with the situation as it is, the best you can, and as the answers come to you and unravel, you continue to manage it without being overwhelmed.

Leylani Cardoso spent more than a decade working in the international retail business dealing with every major retail brand. This experience gave her insight into what today's women look for in a handbag—fashionable, travel-friendly, and refined. With this in mind, Cardoso ventured into a world in which she excelled—designing. The concept of Bolzano was born in 2002 as a result of Cardoso's quest to create the perfect line of "it" handbags for the 21st-century woman. She's an active member of the community and contributes to a multitude of charitable causes for children's needs.

CHAPTER 8
ORGANIZATIONAL STRATEGIES TO IMPROVE PERFORMANCE, PRODUCTIVITY, HEALTH, AND WELL-BEING

In Chapter 5, I described individual strategies that you can effectively use to maximize health while also maximizing performance and productivity at work. Chapter 8 introduces strategies to improve workplace wellness and promote organizational health while growing organizational wealth.

You will benefit substantially from maximizing individual strategies to be at your best on each and every dimension before venturing into improving your organizational health for several reasons. First, you will have hands-on experience as you assess challenges by classifying them within each dimension or distinguishing whether the difficulty relates to health or to the capability of producing wealth. Once you are able to master improvement individually, the organizational component will fall in place easily. First, focus on minimizing any situation that will lead you to burnout (fix the problem); next, increase your energy by implementing effective strategies to maximize your health; and last, improve your well-being on each and every dimension. Believe it or not, once you start to feel better and you experience more energy on your way to enjoy the Power of Wellbeing, you will discover how everything else will seem to align and come together. Your performance and productivity will increase and your contribution at work will follow.

Just as you used AIM I AM on an individual level, you can now use Improve, Achieve, and Maintain as your next strategy to improve a specific area within your organization.

- ☑ AIM
    - ✓ Align
    - ✓ Integrate
    - ✓ Manage your plan
- ☑ I AM
    - ✓ Improve
    - ✓ Achieve
    - ✓ Maintain your goal

Let's say you own a small business and you dislike your corporate culture (emotional dimension). Your workers take time off without asking permission, deadlines are easily dismissed, and chaos has taken over. You saw it coming. You had a strict office manager but few people liked her bossy attitude. Being the "nice guy," you started saying yes to every request to arrive later, leave earlier, extend a deadline, pay in advance, and so on. Although this trouble did not arise overnight, your problems are definitely affecting performance and productivity at work. This is costing you money!

You will first need to improve this situation. The consequences of not doing anything are unsustainable: You have seen an obvious decline in your productivity throughout the past few months, particularly since your office manager decided to leave after she complained that people didn't respect her authority. Now, to continue to get things done, you are the one working overtime, completing unfinished business, and correcting projects halfway done. Maybe your wife has complained that you are no longer coming home for dinner, or maybe your children are not even saying hi to you in the morning. You have a sense of urgency to change this, and you should.

Although you may want to explore why you want to be the good guy, you have little time but to get into action to resolve this problem that may already be costing you hundreds, thousands, hundreds of thousands, or millions of dollars.

The idea is to improve the business culture (emotional dimension) by better defining your goals of the ideal work values you'd like to establish (spiritual dimension). You must break down the overall process into specific goals, achieve each goal, and maintain the goal before going to the next level.

Following this example, you would start to improve from a 0 (absence of work) to, let's say, a 2 (improvement measured by two points up). What activities would you need to implement to go from a 0 to a 2? Well, you could start by clarifying your business expectations regarding work time and taking time off, as well as your sick leave policies. Just clarifying these issues may help you raise two points. You may want to clarify verbally in a special meeting and in writing via a memo. Once you have achieved this goal—that is, of communicating your expectations and managing them when people start asking you for time off— you would maintain this habit for a couple of weeks before moving on to the next step. You may want to give your staff a hint: you will now focus on deadlines and you will expect them to be met. Little by little, you can improve your business culture to create a winning team that works hard and has fun together. In summary, you improved your baseline (moving up two points from 0 to 2), achieved your goal (of changing the business culture to one that takes responsibility for its actions), and maintained your accomplishments (they have become consistent and an integral part of the new culture) before trying to continue to improve. As an example, the scale would look like this:

- ☑ 10: High-functioning organization. Everybody plays by the rules. Special requests are unusual and are always introduced by the employee with a solution in place. Workers are self-motivated to do an outstanding job. The environment is collaborative, with open communication to maximize performance and productivity at work. Policies and procedures are in place but it is unnecessary to discuss them, as the environment shows that good work habits and ethics are obvious within the organization as a whole. Deadlines are met like clockwork. Performance and productivity are at their best. Return on investment is optimal.

221

☑ 9: High-functioning business. People play by the rules. Deadlines are met with high performance and productivity. Workers are self-motivated.

☑ 8: High-functioning business where everybody plays by the rules. People are motivated to do a good job. The quality of the products is very good.

☑ 7: High-functioning business where people play by the rules without needing to be reminded about the rules. There is occasional extension of deadlines or need to correct final projects.

☑ 6: People produce with external motivators and prompting to meet deadlines or correct final projects.

☑ 5: Neutral productivity. Quality is okay but there are errors.

☑ 4: Some projects are completed but many are incomplete. The constant is inconsistency.

☑ 3: A few projects are completed. Poor quality of projects. Actions you could take: Clarify policies and procedures verbally and in writing. Clarify work expectations.

☑ 2: Most projects are not done. Poor quality of projects. Actions you could take: Start over! Clarify policies and procedures verbally and in writing. Clarify work expectations. Be directive. Tell people what to do first, second, and third.

☑ 1: Disorganized; minor things get done. Rules are not clear. Actions you could take: Clarify policies and procedures verbally and in writing.

☑ 0: Corporate culture is chaos: People do whatever they want to do. Rules may be written somewhere but there is no leadership to implement them. You are losing time, energy, and money.

Note that this example addresses the "AIM" component of "AIM I AM": Align, Integrate, and Manage your plan. The AIM component is necessary to understand the significance of these elements when improving one aspect in a comprehensive way.

Many people may implement change with a final goal in mind, but it is the breaking down of this goal to smaller parts that makes the plan feasible and easy to be carried through. A business owner may feel completely overwhelmed when her or his workforce takes over the corporate culture and may feel like giving up altogether, whereas, when breaking the strategy into smaller parts, it becomes much easier to execute one step at a time.

You can establish each goal by setting your ideal goal (10), describing what that attribution means, breaking down each point with its description up to 0 (absence of the desired goal, for example). Next, you would identify your position within the scale. Once you know your baseline, the idea is to improve each section by one or two points. Improve your baseline, Achieve your goal, and Maintain the goal prior to continuing to improve. Continue this strategy until you achieve your ideal goal.

STRATEGIES TO IMPROVE YOUR BUSINESS PERFORMANCE AND PRODUCTIVITY

Strategy #1: Fix What Is Not Working in the Present

As in the individual strategies, it is very appealing to start something new. Many groups find excitement as they approach a new venture, and yet, if their system is not operating at its best, they will eventually be forced to fix whatever is not working well. Just like a launched shuttle aiming for the moon, engineers will need to fix the shuttle on its way if they find a defective circuit onboard. If they don't fix it, their mission won't reach the moon.

You won't achieve your amazing business goals without a smoothly operating workforce. As in the previous example, you will be forced to focus on improving a business culture so that you can meet your project demands and deliver the best level of products or services.

Use AIM I AM. Make your diagnosis: Identify where the problem is within each dimension, repair the problem, and then move on to Improve, Achieve, and Maintain your Goals.

223

Strategy #2: Establish Your Goals

Fixing something that doesn't work is a goal in and of itself. Once it is fixed, you are now free to continue to improve other areas. Identify your goal. Is your goal to increase your productivity?

Once you have established your business goals, narrow them down to a manageable number, prioritize them, establish deadlines, identify all key players, and lay out a plan to achieve each one of them:

1. Identify your goals.
2. Select the most significant ones.
3. Prioritize them.
4. Select the top three and look at the positives and negatives of achieving each goal. Try a SWOT analysis and decide whether you would still choose these three.
5. Finalize your selection.
6. Pick the top three.
7. Lay out a plan of action to achieve these goals. You can use SMART goals.
8. Break the process down to achievable steps.
9. Establish clear deadlines.
10. Identify everyone involved and communicate your vision and plan.

Strategy #3: Prioritize Your Business Goals: Create an Effective and Efficient System

Set up daily, weekly, monthly, quarterly, and annual goals to keep everyone focused on your company's short- and long-term goals. People perform better and are able to improve their accuracy (bull's eye) and precision (consistency) when directions and expectations are clear.

Whether you are in charge of a large, medium, or small organization, or whether you are in charge of a large or small team, focus on assisting everyone to do their best by helping them prioritize in alignment to your overall goals. Train your managers to lay out expectations and follow up on progress. Although many executives and entrepreneurs have performance-improvement meetings at work, few take the time to effectively train their most precious of assets, their workforce! On the other hand, those leaders who are able to guide their workers to accomplish their vision will have amazing results.

1. Communicate with your managers regularly and lay out clear expectations of goals to be achieved.

2. Break down larger goals into smaller ones. Train your managers to do this with their teams.

3. Avoid giving everyone a pile of things to do without setting up priorities and a ranking order to complete first, second, and third.

4. Create a master plan and instruct every business section to create a plan aligned with it.

5. Keep a master calendar and ensure your deadlines are met.

6. Have all routine processes and procedures in place so that you can intervene accordingly in case of emergency or crisis.

7. Guide your managers to effectively manage priorities and create a culture that can resolve challenges as they come.

8. Set regular times when you will evaluate progress and open to feedback for continued improvement.

9. Facilitate a process in which everyone within the organization takes charge of their own area of responsibility. Create ways in which they can see how their contribution affects the benefit for all.

10. Enhance an organizational culture that focuses on priorities as it continues to grow.

> WEEKLY PLANNING: Days 7, 14, 21, 30
> MONTHLY PLANNING: Days 30, 60, 90, 120, 150, 180, 210, 240, 270, 300, 330, and 360
> YEARLY PLANNING: Yearly thereafter

Strategy #4: Leadership Styles

Clearly define the instances when you expect business leaders to make decisions and execute them directly and when they will operate by having meetings and establishing consensus. In general, clear leadership and guidance will be expected during significant change, critical events, and unexpected situations, whereas a more interactive and consensus-based style will be very helpful for creativity processes, growth opportunities, or projects of expansion. Read all the interviews included in this edition. You will learn the significance of staying calm when leading under pressure from Brian Dyson and the significance of efficiency at work from Donna Shalala. You will learn how important it is to be absolutely prepared when launching a new venture from Gary Hoover and how you will face new challenges and need to manage people through tough times from Janet Vergis. You will learn how what you thought you wanted may shift overnight and creat a new opportunity for growth from Marsha Firestone, and how to transform your leadership style from being a firefighter to a strategic leader with Gerry Czarnecki. You will also learn how to face life-changing business needs while managing life events from Leylani Cardoso and how to test your core values from Nando Parrado.

Strategy #5: Start a New Project

Start a new venture or launch a new project when you are on Quadrants 4 (High Health and Low P2) or 3 (High Health and High P2). Quadrant 4 is reflective of a new company whereas Quadrant 3 reflects a high-functioning stage of a successful company.

226

Some specific strategies include:

1. Make sure all processes that could become automatic are in place so as to maximize efficiency and efficacy.

2. Identify one project at a time. Avoid running multiple projects at the same time unless you have opportunities to cross-promote or to integrate the projects.

3. If you need to run multiple projects, pre-plan when you will launch each.

4. Identify all key internal players. Have their 100 percent buy-in prior to your launch.

5. Identify all key external players. Define your strategic approach.

6. Communicate internally to lay out your strategic plan.

7. Lay out your execution plan with clear responsibilities and deadlines.

8. Define specific times to evaluate how the project is going.

9. Be open to immediate suggestions but avoid constantly moving in different directions depending on your feedback. Gather quality advice but make the decision on your own.

10. Evaluate your project upon completion, check the lessons learned, and incorporate them for your next project.

EFFECTIVE STRATEGIES TO MANAGE CRISES

Coping with personal loss, whether it is the loss of a close family friend or family member, or a divorce or financial difficulties, is, to the individual, similar to a product recall, company fraud, leadership misconduct, unethical business deals, or a public scandal to the organization. Both man-made and natural catastrophes may destroy the foundation of an organization. A whole country was impacted upon when a plane carrying the

227

Polish president and Poland's top 10 percent leadership crashed in Russia in April 2010. Several companies disappeared on 9/11. Politicians', athletes', and businessmen's love affairs impacted upon careers and organizations, costing millions of dollars in lost sponsorships and their positions of power. A company may be struck by crisis when its major client goes under or when a key executive is kidnapped. Although there are many ways to resolve the issue at stake it is of essence to manage critical situations focusing on people first. Even when thousands or millions of dollars are lost when business goes down, people will always remember how the company managed its people and how it related to other people through tough situations.

The following are general effective strategies I have used in my work as a corporate consultant in critical incidents. Although they are useful tips within the crisis management, they are also useful during calm times.

Strategy #6: Assess the Situation

Ensure your workers' safety first when facing an unexpected event. Manage your emotions first and focus on staying calm. Your workforce will look up to you for guidance. Establish a "range of emergency situations," so as to react accordingly. You want to avoid responding to any difficulty as if the world were coming to an end. Keep things in perspective: Look at the whole picture and avoid interpreting crises as overwhelming.

Choose your top managers and give them tasks to do. Lead by example. Share your expectation of ensuring they also manage their emotions and stay calm. If you have a plan in place, follow the plan. Otherwise, assess your situation:

1. Is everyone okay?
2. Let's check all systems. What is working well and what needs to be fixed?
3. What needs immediate attention and what can wait?
4. Who's going to fix what needs immediate attention?

5. How will we communicate our findings? How will we manage expectations?

6. What is the human impact of the crisis?

7. What is the immediate financial loss? What is the long-term loss?

8. What can we do to have the best possible outcome in spite of the challenging situation?

9. How can we cross-collaborate to minimize loss?

10. How is the public responding to our reaction?

Strategy #7: Concentrate on the Here and Now

The best way to react in times of crisis is to be in great shape on a regular basis. The more robust your business is, the easier it will be to bounce back. Focus on what needs immediate attention and avoid patching a problem if you feel it will only come back to haunt you later. Help everyone focus on the here and now. Repair and fix now with a watchful eye on the future. Find exactly where your company stands during the critical moment. If you have a plan in place, go to it immediately and get everyone involved. Assign activities and actions to everyone and lead the way to resolving the situation assertively and steadily. If you do not have a plan in place, create a crisis team and work through the crisis together. Organize discussions so as to resolve the problem together, take notes, and use them as a template for future planning.

Strategy #8: Go Back to Your Schedule or Plan as Soon as Possible

Start with the simplest routine and go back to your processes and procedures. Break down processes into simple steps if needed. Instruct leaders and managers to go back to your business plan. This plan should be easily available, as, during times of crisis or personal loss (or both), it may be difficult to remember exactly what the next step was. Maintain a positive attitude about

229

your ability to solve the situation and promote this attitude with your leaders. Look for opportunities to grow beyond just resolving the problem. Make relevant decisions that relate to your here and now. Move forward as you immerse yourself in change. Avoid spending too much time going over what happened. It is best to focus on the lessons learned looking toward the future.

Strategy #9 Avoid Making Big Changes During Times of Crisis

Make relevant changes that affect your business in the here and now and avoid making drastic changes during times of crisis. Take the time to conduct an assessment of the situation and look at the positive or negative outcomes with each action you want to undertake. With more time, conduct a SWOT analysis, addressing the strengths, weaknesses, opportunities, and threats of each further action.

Strategy #10: Approach Your Trusted Circle and Establish Significant Relationships Beyond Your Comfort Group

Gather your board and build consensus on sensitive decisions that could have a large impact on your business or your workforce. Avoid isolating and instead create a strong bond with your trusted circle of business partners, leaders, and managers. Learn exactly what each can offer. Distribute responsibilities within this trusted group, and lay out the actions to be performed.

Allow cross-collaboration within the business and with outside clients that may also be struggling. Having an extended networking group will assist your business to recover faster than if you were on your own. Many business owners survived the recession by joining forces and sharing staff members, for example. Move toward your business goals and cross-collaborate with other businesses to create WIN-WIN-WIN solutions. Ask each of your employees to contact three clients they know on a daily basis as you are trying to bounce back from the critical situation.

Strategy #11: Assess Your Intervention

Evaluate what worked and what didn't work for your business. Improve your overall plan and continue to plan ahead. Consider this an opportunity to continue to improve your business and to simplify as much of the process as possible. Although many executives expect a magic solution to resolve a time of crisis, the most effective strategies still entail being consistently organized on a regular basis. Keep hope alive. As entrepreneurs leading your companies or executives leading and managing your work group, others will look up to you to lead them during times of crisis. This does not mean you have to do it alone. Share your hope and concerns with others as you move forward. This sharing will not only inspire others but will also refuel your own energy as you move forward. Lead by example and promote this approach with each of your managers within your business.

STRATEGIES TO IMPROVE ORGANIZATIONAL HEALTH & WELL-BEING

Lessons Learned From the Healthy Organization and From the Health & Wealth Matrix

1. Define the healthy organization as multidimensional.

2. Think of the organization as a core of dimensions in full alignment: physical, emotional, intellectual, social, and spiritual. Your business's ability to perform at its best within each dimension is measured by its performance and productivity within each dimension.

3. Set up efficient systems and transcribe them in clear policies and procedures.

4. Create healthy habits within the organization and practice them daily. Be consistent.

5. Create a healthy corporate culture and invite everyone to be an integral part of the organization. Lead by

231

example. Create an organization that is well-known as a source of health and wellness to all its workforce, clients, and customers.

6. Establish your baseline health and improve from there.

7. Establish your health priorities: Fix what needs to be fixed first and then improve.

8. If you have to fix several areas, ask for help to establish which to do first, second, and third.

9. Create the 10-step health improvement scale and focus on one area you are trying to fix and improve. Use Improve, Achieve, and Maintain your goal as a model.

10. Spread your timelines so that you can track your improvement over time.

Strategies to Improve Physical Health

1. Find the right location for your business. Plan ahead of expanding to new locations. What are the benefits and the risks of staying where you are, moving, or expanding? How much space do you need to start? How much space will you need in the near future?

2. Build a solid foundation to promote productivity at work. Create a safe work environment where people can achieve their best. Offer all necessary equipment and tools to perform at the highest level.

3. Bring quality people to support your business goals. This will prove to be your most valuable strategy to succeed. Do you need to hire people to work directly with you, or would you outsource?

4. Create a strong organization by appointing key people to key positions. Even if you start on your own, have the end in mind. What will your organization look like when you grow? Communicate the organizational layout to all players.

5. Create simple and clear policies and procedures. Foster a work environment where everyone knows what they should do at all times.

6. Provide the appropriate technological foundation and support. Ensure you have what you need but not too much to distract. We don't know what we would do without our cellular phones, PDAs, or constant access to e-mail or the Internet these days, but ensure this supports and doesn't sidetrack from productivity at work.

7. Create integrated systems including a solid work environment, the appropriate technology, communication support, and, most important of all, the right people at work.

8. Minimize waste: Why spend $10,000 on a coffee table instead of $250 if you could invest $10,000 in equipment that will make you money?

9. Maximize your return: create relevant ways to generate revenue. Keep impeccable finances and a strong image of being a highly credible, honest, and competent organization.

10. Create your mission statement after clarifying your values (spiritual dimension) and establishing your vision for the future (intellectual dimension). Communicate your mission across your organization and transform it into action.

Strategies to Improve Emotional Health

1. Assess your company baseline state of emotional health. Is there one attitude that prevails?

2. Set up the priority to improve your corporate culture if the prevalent mood is negative (constant criticizing, bickering, backstabbing, or acting out). If the prevalent mood has been negative for months or years it may take you time to shift into a positive mode. The earlier you start, the easier it gets; the easier it gets, the better it gets.

3. If there is a problem within the emotional dimension, set up a plan to fix it. Unhappy people at work won't perform or produce at their highest level and could become a toxic influence, further impacting upon the overall productivity within an organization.

4. Create positive streams of communication among leadership, management, and employees.

5. Consider an open-door policy but also set up regular meeting times with your direct reports.

6. Have regular meetings that work for you. Have a clear agenda with a beginning, middle, and an end with a plan of action and deadline expectations. Manage your time: An hourly meeting can't go for hours.

7. Enhance positive interactions within the workplace and across teams. Create an environment of camaraderie and collaboration. Avoid unnecessary competition within the organization. The "I win, you lose" mentality creates friction and decreases performance and productivity. Instead, promote "We both win" when working on a joint project.

8. Reward positive behavior and set up clear consequences when inappropriate behavior occurs. Have a zero-tolerance attitude with bullying and disrespect of any type (overt comments against people because of gender, sexual orientation, race, ethnicity, or social status).

9. Enhance a calm and proactive attitude of getting things done in advance in contrast to doing everything at the last minute. This will help your employees be active and relaxed instead of working under constant—unnecessary—stress. Have clear protocols for critical events and go back to your regular schedule as soon as the crisis is resolved.

10. Create an environment where people love to come to work. Inspire others to join you in your common goals and take time to celebrate your success.

Strategies to Improve Cognitive Health

1. Assess your company's baseline state of cognitive or intellectual health.

2. Establish your improvement scale from 0 to 10 (ideal state).

3. Create your vision for the organization after identifying your values and source of inspiration (spiritual dimension). Communicate your vision and create a strategy to carry your mission into action (physical dimension).

4. Identify key learning areas that would enhance performance and productivity at work.

5. Create comprehensive ways to learn. Some people are visual learners, others are auditory learners, and still others are kinesthetic learners. Avoid endless presentations with no participation. Integrate interactive learning programs within your organization.

6. Promote a culture that values learning and improvement.

7. Create clear paths to advance within the organization. Motivate your employees to continue to improve for their own benefit, for the benefit of the organization, and for the benefit of their clients.

8. Generate exciting ways to learn that are pertinent to the profession, generation, or culture. Expose your workforce to new ways of learning and ask for feedback to see what works best.

9. Create Power Breaks within the organization. This may include taking a break during which people can listen to music, relax, or exercise. This will enhance creativity and productivity.

10. Avoid overworking your workforce to exhaustion. Although working many hours can enhance performance and productivity, working *too many* hours will lead to burnout and decreased performance and productivity.

Strategies to Improve Social Health

1. Assess your baseline state of social health.

2. Establish your improvement scale from 0 to 10 (ideal state).

235

3. Create an organizational culture with an active role in the community. Enhance an image with a company personality that is consistent at each and every event.

4. Create positive interactions with local companies.

5. Create positive interactions with competitors. Focus on creating strategies to enhance your products or services rather than destroying your competitors'. Focus on "your good" rather than "their bad."

6. Create opportunities to cross-collaborate with other companies to impact upon your community.

7. Create relationships across your obvious market. Even if your company conducts business-to-business transactions, create ties to schools, religious entities, the government, the military, and nonprofits.

8. Ensure you always have company representation at major events.

9. Get involved in philanthropic and charity events. Give back to the community at large.

10. Create good balance between your company involvement and alignment with your company values, vision, and mission.

Strategies to Improve Spiritual Health

1. Assess your baseline state of spiritual health.

2. Establish your improvement scale starting from 0 to 10 (an ideal state such as experiencing The Power of Wellbeing).

3. Identify, clarify, and describe the values that are important to the company (founder, leader, and board). Make a list of five to 10 values. Decide to live and abide by these values. These values should inspire you to do what you do: produce products or services that enhance other peoples' lives in some way. Establish strong ethical guidelines to work creatively, but living by the rules at the same time.

4. Find your experiences where these values are completely aligned and mark other instances in which you believe they are not. Set up a plan to improve those values that are not in alignment. For example, if you value respect for people and you have a bully in the company, you will need to create a plan to share your expectations, clarify the consequences, and expect 100 percent commitment, tracking progress.

5. Avoid hiring or retaining people who are constantly breaking the rules, people who don't seem to care about anyone but themselves, and people who are not aligned with your values. Without judging them, realize your values are not aligned with theirs and this is not a good work match. Give the person a chance to choose to stay if he or she commits to follow and live by the company values. Let the person go if he or she doesn't. Avoid making high performers "indispensable" when their behavior is unacceptable. Interestingly, many people misbehave in the workplace because they can! When you set boundaries that would enhance a positive workplace environment, those who were acting out may transform their act and blend in properly if they truly want to stay and "play in the sandbox." Others who want to continue to ostracize their coworkers will leave when they can't continue to bully other people.

6. Avoid focusing on negative information, gossip, or ongoing criticism, or doing anything that is not aligned with your values or spiritual source. Avoid listening to negative conversations or starting interactions with a negative attitude.

7. Include artistic activities where your workforce has the opportunity to contemplate art in each and every form: visual (painting), auditory (music), or performance (theater, dance, and opera), to name a few. This will help enhance creativity and productivity in the workplace.

8. Find actions, experiences, and interactions that inspire your workforce to improve.

9. Create a culture that wants to contribute to a good cause: Welcome philanthropic or charity events. Volunteer as an organization for special projects that are aligned with your values.

10. Avoid judging others for their lifestyle choices, age, gender, race, social background, or level of education. Create an environment where everyone who can make a positive contribution is welcome. Promote health and wellness in the workplace and enjoy The Power of Wellbeing.

Figure 26: Write Your Own Healthy Strategies

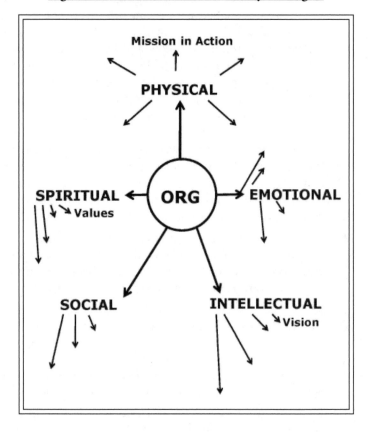

Interview 8

"Live"
NANDO PARRADO

Born and raised in Uruguay, Nando Parrado made a trip to Chile to participate in an international rugby tournament in 1972. The plane crashed tragically at 18,000 feet in the Andes Mountains. His mother and younger sister died in the accident. Nando survived 72 days in what few human beings can even imagine, masterminding an 11-day rescue mission with his friend, Roberto Canessa. Both worked with Piers Paul Read to write the world bestseller, *Alive*. A movie followed 20 years later. Ethan Hawke played his character.

NANDO PARRADO ON LEADING UNDER PRESSURE

Cora: *I have interviewed many people who have experienced instances of leading under pressure, but I don't think I've ever spoken to anyone who has gone through the kind of pressure you have. Can you tell me about that?*

Parrado: I can tell you that I had all the pressure I could sustain in my life in my early years. Everything in the last 37 years has been a joy compared with what I went through, so any pressure in business is just issues, just simple things. The highest, most profound pressure I've ever felt is when you fight for your life and you know you're going to die. What can you compare it to? Right now, it's your company! If you lose your company, okay, you can go paint houses or wash cars. But your *life*... When people tell me, "Oh, I have so much stress! I have to finish this project." Or, "My sales have dropped 35 percent," so what?

You have this perspective that very few people have and are unlikely to experience in their lifetimes. Tell me more about the perspective you have on life.

We learned, when we were very young, and we suffered, when we were very young, types of pressure and fear that are only comparable to when you're in war, or a concentration camp, or facing a firing squad. Everything I have faced afterwards, people say, "How can you do so many things?" Because they are so easy compared to what I have done. I have to face people; who cares? It's a human being. I have to make a project. It's only a project. If it fails, I start another one. I've never felt fear afterwards. I think I've used all the amount of fear I've had; my fear batteries were exhausted then. Because I lived with fear 24 hours a day, physical fear.

In a way, after surviving, you get an amount of knowledge in fear, in pressure, and in stress, that when you compare that to everyday life issues—and luckily we can compare—then we say, "Okay, this is just an issue, it's not a problem," and things happen in life. You have financial crisis, economic crisis, relationship crisis, you have the loss of a dear friend or family member, but all those things happen. I don't ask myself why, I just go forward. If you look back, all you get is a bloody pain in the neck.

In the United States, for example, people are attached to success. If you're not successful, you're not happy. But for me, happiness is the road to success. I might not achieve it *ever*. I might not ever achieve it! Maybe people who don't travel around the world, they don't see how blessed they are to have a job, to drive a car, to sleep on a bed every night...that's a blessing. Not to be rich or to be attached to success. Everybody wants to imitate Richard Branson, Bill Gates, all these guys, but there are only three, four, five, six in the world. How many millions of people, in the world—in Asia, in Africa, in the United States, in South America—are trying to achieve success? And very few do, if you measure success in monetary ways, in money. But you can be very rich on the way to attain that success that you'll never obtain, if you're happy with your family, with your friends, with your life.

Have you seen a change in how you look at happiness and your inner peace?

I have refined without knowing, and I have achieved, for me, a wellbeing that's perfect. I can say without fear, to the most important CEO in the world of the biggest company, that I prefer to go to the beach with my dogs early in the morning than to go to the office. *Then* I go to the office. If I [went] to the office two hours earlier, I'd be richer, maybe because I'd make another business. But I will lose those two hours with my dogs. Which is more important? For *me*, those two hours with my dogs! And people might say, "Okay, you can do that because you're well off." No, I'm not that well off. I'm well off because I want to be well off with my life and my family.

Maybe you are well off because you're spending your time with the dogs and that makes you happy.

Yeah, that makes me happy. If I look that I have, instead of going to the beach with the dogs, 10,000 more dollars in the bank, would that make me happier? No.

I have worked hard also. I work hard, I produce TV programs, I have my hardware store businesses, and I have a cable station...I work hard but I try to enjoy those moments also. I don't try to look for problems and stress, and if something arises and someone comes running into my office, "Oh! We have this problem!" I say, "Okay, you'll find a solution. We'll find the solution to that, but don't worry, it's only a business."

Do you set up as a goal to experience joy and be happy every single time, or does this come naturally?

Oh, naturally, I don't think about it; I don't work on it. It comes naturally because I know I am blessed with being alive again. I should enjoy this life. It would be a crime not to enjoy this life. What should I do? Would I commit myself to social work all the days of my life? No. I help some people whenever I can, I help people in my family, but I enjoy life. I want to be with the people I love.

LEADING UNDER PRESSURE

What is it that you enjoy the most these days?

These days, I enjoy being free, having the time to go with my dogs to the beach, being with my family—anticipating the joy of meeting my two girls in Barcelona in 10 days' time. Because I have learned that the most important thing in the world is the affections, not the money. Imagine if you're in front of a firing squad or someone is going to be thrown in an oven in a concentration camp, are you going to think about the money you left in the bank? About your computer or your fax machine? The next project that is in your mind? No, you think about the people that you're going to miss because you're going to die. We have learned that when we were very young. I could lie to *you*...but not to me. If I lied to me, I would be so stupid. I would have died. If I had lied to myself.

Given the circumstances that helped you rise to the occasion, it was very obvious that you were looking forward and not looking back.

I think I'm very pragmatic when people ask me about *what's God's responsibility* or *what did I do in my ordeal*. He didn't do anything! It happened! The pilot made a mistake! We crashed! Do you think that every time a car crashes on I-95, you think it was God's will every time? No! The guy was talking on his mobile phone and he didn't see the guy brake in front of him and he crashed.

From all of this, it sounds as if you've really lived your life without fear.

I lived my life without...not fear; how can I say it...I fought so much for my life that I wanted to experience my life. I didn't do drugs. I don't drink alcohol because I was a sportsman, but I drink wine now. I never went beyond what a normal guy does. I did my sports, I raced cars, boats, whatever; I worked hard. I never had the necessity to smoke pot or do drugs or cocaine. What for? Life is so interesting without those things.

For me, it's my family first, my friends are second, my dogs are third, my sports are fourth, and my businesses are in *fifth place*. It's very clear, in my conferences, in everything—"Don't lose connections: Don't lose the connections with your family and your friends because in times of need, that's what's really valuable."

Is there any message that you really want to get across to people, either a question no one asked you but you wish someone had, or some message that you think is important?

I can only relate to my experience and what I feel and what I do. I see people who are stressed or have problems. They have economy problems, they lose a job—I understand those things, but that's part of life. Everybody wants life to be perfect. The ambition, the will of everybody is to live a perfect life, but it's like a puzzle: You have different pieces and sometimes a bad piece gets dropped into your life. You have to go forward. Nobody will help you except you. When difficult times come, you have to make decisions. You have to be the captain of your own life. If you're blessed, if somebody will buy your book, maybe they have money to buy that book. Or they will be sleeping on a bed, or they will be drinking water, or they will be eating. *That* is a blessing! It's a fantastic blessing. Only seeing that, that's a blessing. If you see the millions and millions of people who live with less than one dollar a day, you will never ever complain.

Nando Parrado is a successful businessman and an active sportsman. He's married to Veronique and is the proud father of two daughters, Verónica and Cecilia. He is the president of the family company **Seler Parrado S.A.** and the founder of a cable television company and two television media production enterprises. Nando travels the world as an international speaker, helping people unlock their potential and excellence in the workplace and everyday life. He's the author of the bestseller *Miracle in the Andes*. Nando was selected as "The Keynote Speaker" for the IASB (International Association of Speakers' Bureaus) in 2007. In 2009, he was the keynote speaker for the closing at the NSA convention (National Speakers' Association) with an unforgettable standing ovation.

APPENDIX

LIFE-WORK ASSESSMENT

Use the grids on the following page to rate your current level on each and every individual and organizational dimension starting with 0 (absence) to 10 (ideal). Use the strategy of advancing by one or two points up within the dimension where you would like to improve until you reach your desired goal. Check your progress by following up at regular intervals.

INDIVIDUAL

10					
9					
8					
7					
6					
5					
4					
3					
2					
1					
0					
	PHYSICAL	INTELLECTUAL	EMOTIONAL	SPIRITUAL	SOCIAL

ORGANIZATION

10					
9					
8					
7					
6					
5					
4					
3					
2					
1					
0					
	PHYSICAL	INTELLECTUAL	EMOTIONAL	SPIRITUAL	SOCIAL

INDEX

LEADING UNDER PRESSURE

LEADING UNDER PRESSURE

ABOUT THE AUTHOR

Dr. Gaby Cora is president and founder of The Executive Health & Wealth Institute and managing partner of The Florida Neuroscience Center. She is the author of The Power of Wellbeing Series: *Leading Under Pressure*, *Managing Work in Life*, *Quantum Wellbeing*, and the provocative *Alpha Female Leader*. A Renaissance woman, Dr. Cora is a medical doctor with a master's in business administration, a major in healthcare administration and policy, and is a board-certified psychiatrist, psychotherapist, pharmacologist, certified mediator, corporate consultant, wellness coach, professional speaker, spouse, and mother of two young adults. Her areas of expertise include the integration of health and wealth strategies, including the full range of health and disease in mood and anxiety disorders (depression, bipolar disorder, OCD, panic disorder, and post-traumatic stress disorder), stress management, and burnout prevention. She's a professional member of the National Speakers' Association, and she's a regular guest on radio and television shows talking about leadership, management, mental health, health, and wellness. Dr. Cora has been interviewed on CNN, FOX, and Lifetime, as well as in the *New York Times*, *Chicago Tribune*, *Forbes*, *Business Week*, and *Women Entrepreneur*. Additionally, she has authored scientific papers and has coauthored chapters in medical textbooks on depression and anxiety disorders. Dr. Cora serves as a trustee on the Board of Directors of the American Psychiatric

Foundation and she's the Miami Chapter chair in the Women Presidents' Organization.

Dr. Cora consults Fortune 500 companies and international organizations including The Coca-Cola Company, The World Bank, New York Life, and the pharmaceutical industry. She has consulted and given presentations in the Americas, Europe, Africa, and Asia. Dr. Cora coaches C-level executives and entrepreneurs. Prior to starting Executive Health & Wealth, she was director and Regional Medical Research Specialist for Pfizer Pharmaceuticals and served on the SouthEast Regional Sales Council (seven states). She joined Pfizer after being a clinical researcher at the prestigious National Institutes of Health, where she served in the U.S. Public Health Service. As a clinical researcher, she headed the Obsessive-Compulsive Disorder Unit Research Clinic, building a highly specialized clinical team and conducting state-of-the-art research, which resulted in cutting-edge treatment options and peer-reviewed publications. At the NIH, she served in the Institutional Review Board and received the Hannah Cashman Memorial Award in recognition of her dedicated and compassionate care, given by the Consultation Liaison service at NIMH.

Dr. Cora pursued a research career after her residency in psychiatry at Saint Elizabeth's Hospital and George Washington University in Washington, D.C. She's a graduate of the Executive MBA for Healthcare Professionals program at the University of Miami (2005), and she graduated as a medical doctor at the Universidad de Buenos Aires in Argentina (1989). She completed a trilingual baccalaureate at Barker College in Argentina, graduating valedictorian. She received her School Certification from Cambridge, England. Dr. Cora is fluent in English, Spanish, and French. Of Italian descent, Dr. Cora was born in Brooklyn, New York, and moved to Argentina with her family. Dr. Cora lived in Silver Spring, Maryland, for a decade, and she has lived in Miami, Florida, for another decade. She lives with her husband of 20 years, Eduardo Locatelli, MD, MPH, and their Border collies. Dr. Cora enjoys traveling the world as she gives talks, spending time with her adult children, enjoying the company of her family and friends, playing with her dogs, and water skiing in Key Biscayne.